THE CATILINARIAN CONSPIRACY
IN ITS CONTEXT:
A RE-STUDY OF THE EVIDENCE

AMS PRESS
NEW YORK

THE CATILINARIAN CONSPIRACY
IN ITS CONTEXT:
A RE-STUDY OF THE EVIDENCE

By E. G. HARDY, M.A., D.LITT.

(PRINCIPAL OF JESUS COLLEGE, OXFORD)

BASIL BLACKWELL
OXFORD
1924

2371757

Library of Congress Cataloging in Publication Data

Hardy, Ernest George, 1852-1925.
   The Catilinarian conspiracy in its context.

   Reprint of the 1924 ed. published by B. Blackwell,
Oxford.
   Includes Index.
   1. Rome—History—Conspiracy of Catiline, 65-62 B.C.
   I. Title.
DG259.H3   1976   937'.05   75-41128
ISBN 0-404-14549-3

Reprinted from an original in the collections of the
University of Iowa Library.
From the edition of 1924, Oxford.
First AMS edition published in 1976.
Manufactured in the United States of America

AMS PRESS INC.
NEW YORK, N.Y.

PREFACE

I AM indebted to the courtesy of the Editors of the *Journal of Roman Studies* for allowing me to republish this essay on the Catilinarian Conspiracy in its Context. I have added the last words to the title of the book, because it has been my aim in reconstructing the familiar story to make the conspiracy and its more immediate antecedents occupy a distinct and intelligible place in the history of the political situation between 67 and 63 B.C. Not the least important or difficult of the questions involved is that concerned with the attitude of Caesar and Crassus, and the part played by these statesmen throughout the whole episode. I have ventured to put forward what I believe to be a new explanation of that reserved and guarded attitude on their part, which has led some historians, both ancient and modern, to suspect them of sympathy with Catiline's designs. The book is literally a re-study of the evidence. I have based my narrative solely on the statements of Sallust, Cicero, Plutarch, Appian and Dio Cassius. In most cases these statements have been cited in full. I have carefully avoided anything like a controversial treatment of the subject, and as a matter of fact, I have neither used nor alluded to any modern account or reconstruction of the conspiracy.

Jesus College, Oxford.
   May 25, 1924.

CONTENTS

I.

Crassus, Caesar and Catiline to the end of 66

THE year 63 has always been regarded as Cicero's year, the year in which he gained some of his most striking political successes, and in the course of which he saved the republic. Nevertheless a careful scrutiny of the evidence will convince an impartial observer that, with all his hopes of proving himself a *consul popularis*, Cicero was throughout the year on the defensive, that the initiative was never for a moment in his hands, and therefore that in determining the real causes of the excitements and crises which shook Rome during his consulship we must search for other agents more truly responsible for the issue of events than anything that Cicero said or planned or carried into action.

There was, as appears in many ways not only in this but in previous years, an uneasy suspicion, sometimes amounting to openly expressed belief, that the course of events was being controlled by powerful figures in the background. But while there was this impression, there was also a disposition among responsible men to apply the prudent rule of mentioning no names. On the other hand, modern historians, in trying to interpret the significance of the year's events, have no such motive for reticence, and one would think it inevitable that the names of Crassus and Caesar should figure more prominently in the history of these years, and not least of the second half of 63, than they are made to do by either Cicero or Sallust.

I have already attempted[1] to trace the purposes and policy of Caesar at the beginning of 63 as manifested in the agrarian law proposed by Rullus, and the impeachment of Rabirius for *perduellio*. There can be no doubt that Caesar, though in the background, was not only the

[1] See *Journal of Philology*, xxxiii, 64, and xxxiv, 67.

prime mover in both these episodes, but that they were both intended in different ways to play an important part in shaping the general situation, and in strengthening the position of the popular leaders in their relations to Pompey, to the senatorial government and to the *plebs urbana*. If we add to these two absorbing incidents the abrogation by Labienus of the *lex Cornelia de sacerdotiis*, and the revival of the *lex Domitia*, with the result that Caesar was elected *pontifex maximus*,[1] it will be abundantly clear that during the first three or four months of the year Caesar, though always through the instrumentality of others, was in reality attempting to dominate the situation. It is true that, owing to tactical mistakes, he had failed to accomplish his object, entirely in the matter of the agrarian law, largely in that of Rabirius, but it is hard to believe that these two checks would have caused him to subside for the rest of the year into a position of retirement and inactivity. The events of the next six months were not only full of public excitement, but raised questions of vital moment both to Crassus as a financier, and to Caesar as a politician. This can hardly be denied, and yet in most accounts, ancient and modern, of the Catilinarian conspiracy the two most influential men in Rome are represented as playing the part of mere spectators, leaving these vital interests to be decided by Catiline and his irresponsible associates on the one hand, and on the other by Cicero, whose action at the beginning of the year had shown him to be Pompeian, senatorial and anti-popular in his aims and sympathies. That the names of Crassus and Caesar should have been as far as possible kept out of sight at the time is intelligible, and even the later writers were content in the main to hand on the story as Cicero himself had recounted it, though some of them, as we shall see, occasionally made use of other contemporary or nearly contemporary authorities who were not equally reticent.

---

[1] Dio Cassius (xxxvii, 37) places this after the execution of the Catilinarians, but it obviously happened in the earlier half of the year.

The reconstruction, however, of political situations by taking into account the more obscure agencies and less obvious motives did not in the eyes of Plutarch or Dio Cassius, still less of Suetonius and Appian, fall within the historian's task, though Dio at least is clear-sighted enough to reject the false situation suggested by Sallust. It is precisely with these reconstructions that the modern historian is concerned, and where no new evidence is forthcoming, they must always contain an element of hypothesis, to justify which there must be a careful re-sifting and re-interpretation of the existing authorities. In the present case such a reconstruction has been attempted again and again, and all students of Roman history are familiar with the narratives of Mommsen, Strachan-Davidson, Heitland and Ferrero. It is not my intention to criticise or even to refer to any of these accounts. I will only say that they none of them furnish an explanation which satisfies me of the reserved and even detached position of the two popular leaders during the last six months of 63. I have no hypothesis to start with, but I feel sure that to reach one the conspiracy must be examined in its context, and that the situation, of which it was an incident, must be made to begin in 67 or 66. I have for several reasons abstained entirely from consulting the monographs of John, von Stern and Schwartz, with whose conclusions I am unacquainted, and I go back entirely to the original authorities.

I have used the term ' leaders of the popular party ' to describe Crassus and Caesar in 63, and I should so describe them from 65 onwards. But it must be remembered that the popular party recovered only gradually from the effects of the Sullan régime. Undoubtedly the first consulship of Pompey and Crassus had marked a popular coalition and some details of the 'Gracchan constitution' had been restored. It is equally true that Pompey's position in the East, as defined by the laws of Gabinius and Manilius, had emanated from the popular party. But the leadership of that party was complicated through the unfriendly personal relations of Crassus to Pompey. Partly through these, partly through his comparative indifference to politics, we do not find Crassus actively directing the party until well after Pompey's departure.

There was no one, however, so powerful or influential on the anti-senatorial side, and when we find in the course of 67 a series of important popular laws passed by the tribune Cornelius, it is impossible to suppose that they were not sanctioned, even if they were not actually supported, by Crassus. We know from Asconius' commentary on Cicero's lost speech *pro Cornelio* how bitter senatorial feeling was against the tribune, what obstruction was put in his way, and how a charge of *maiestas* was brought against him.[1] There seems some reason to think that Manilius, one of the tribunes for 66, was to have carried on the work of Cornelius. He at any rate was ready immediately on entering office with a sweeping measure on the freedman vote, and it was one of the charges against Cornelius that he had passed on this law to his successor.[2] But Manilius was a weaker man than Cornelius, and the law, though it might commend itself to popular leaders anxious about votes, was not so welcome to free-born citizens, and the senate with popular approval was able to compel its withdrawal. On this, according to Dio Cassius (xxxvi, 42), ἐπειδὴ τὸ πλῆθος δεινῶς ἠγανάκτει, τὰ μὲν πρῶτα ἔς τε τὸν Κράσσον καὶ ἐς ἄλλους τινὰς τὴν γνώμην ἀνῆγεν, and then, when no one believed him, sought

---

[1] According to Asconius the Cornelian laws were : (1) *ne quis legatis exterarum nationum pecuniam expensam ferret ;* (2) *ne quis in senatu legibus solveretur nisi CC adfuissent, neve quis, cum solutus esset, intercederet, cum de ea re ad populum ferretur ;* (3) *ut praetores ex edictis suis perpetuis ius dicerent* (in Cornel., 58-60, Dio Cass. xxxvi, 39 and 40). It appears from D. C. c. 38 that even the *lex Calpurnia de ambitu* was only a milder version, substituted by the senate, of a severer measure prepared by Cornelius.

[2] Asconius (64) quotes as Cicero's words : *legem, inquit, de libertinorum suffragiis Cornelius C. Manilio dedit.* Cicero's reply to the charge would not seem to have been very convincing.

to gain popularity by his proposal for extending
Pompey's command. I would not press too far this
reference to Crassus, but in some of his authorities Dio
must have found the name of Crassus in this connexion,
and putting this statement side by side with the fragment
from Cicero, we get a slight indication of what on general
grounds we might have expected, that both Cornelius and
Manilius had some sort of political connexion with Crassus.

Caesar's position was of course so far less clearly defined.
He had, however, already made his mark as a man from
whom the popular party might expect much, and it was
in 67 that, returning from his quaestorship in Spain, he
gave unmistakable encouragement to the Latin colonies
of the Transpadane region in their agitation for the full
franchise.[1] From 66 at any rate there began to be signs
that he and Crassus were working together, for in the
summer of that year he was elected aedile ; and this with
the lavish expenditure foreshadowed implied unlimited
financial support which can hardly have come from any
source but Crassus. It was probably, as Dio suggests,[2]
from no goodwill to Pompey, but from a desire not to spoil
his chances of election by the people, that Caesar supported,
as Crassus almost certainly did not, the notorious *lex
Manilia*. We may indeed safely assume that, from the
moment that law was passed, the looming danger of a
military dictatorship must have been patent to Caesar
and Crassus, and equally distasteful to both.

It is probable that Caesar's election as aedile was not
the only election in the summer of 66 in which Crassus was
interested. There was a keen contest for the consulship,
and as the result, Autronius Paetus and P. Sulla were
elected. There is no evidence, apart from any presumption
from the events at the end of the year, that either Autronius or Sulla had as yet any political connexion with
Crassus and Caesar, though they were probably known to
be on the popular rather than the senatorial side. At any
rate large sums of money must have been forthcoming to

[1] Suet. *Iul.* 8.   [2] Dio Cass. xxxvi, 43.

secure their election, as they were soon after accused of bribery under the *lex Calpurnia* by L. Cotta and L. Torquatus, and though Autronius tried to interfere with the court by means of gladiators (*pro Sull.* 16), both were condemned and unseated.[1] This necessitated a second election in the autumn, and on this second occasion Catiline wished to be a candidate. That Catiline's candidature was at the second and not at the ordinary election is proved by Sallust (c. 18), who, after mentioning the condemnation of Autronius and Sulla, goes on : *post paulo Catilina pecuniarum repetundarum reus prohibitus erat consulatum petere quod intra legitimos dies profiteri nequiverit.* The passage shows, as we shall see, some misconception on Sallust's part, but I cite it here because the words *post paulo* in the context rule out the first or ordinary consular elections.

Now though there is no direct evidence that Catiline came forward in the anti-senatorial interest, the action taken by the senate was very remarkable and must have had some special cause. Catiline had recently returned from governing Africa after his praetorship, and it appears that, before his arrival in Rome, envoys from Africa had already made charges against him in the senate, which, on this *ex parte* evidence, passed some severe decrees against him, and in Cicero's words *te auctoritate sua spoliatum ornamentis omnibus paene vinctum Africanis oratoribus tradiderunt.*[2] Not only so ; but when Volcacius Tullus the consul consulted the leading senators as to whether he should accept Catiline's candidature, the decision was

---

[1] The trial and condemnation of Autronius and Sulla are given by Asconius, 75; Sallust, *Cat.* 18; Dio Cassius, xxxvi, 44. There is some doubt whether the Torquatus who accused Sulla was the father or the son. Asconius and Dio make him the father, who took his place as consul, but a passage of Cicero (*de fin.* ii, 19, 62) is against this. In *pro Sull.* 49 Cicero's words to the younger Torquatus leave the matter doubtful : *adflicto P. Sulla consulatus vobis pariebatur.*

[2] The words are quoted by Asconius, 89 ; conf. 85 : *gravissimis vestris decretis notatus est.*

against him : *qui (principes civitatis) cum L. Volcacio cos. in consilio fuissent, ne petendi quidem potestatem tibi esse voluerunt.* These are Cicero's own words, but Asconius (89) explains more fully. After Catiline had returned to seek the consulship, and the envoys had made complaints in the senate, *professus deinde est* (the word clearly being used in a non-technical sense) *Catilina petere se consulatum. L. Volcacius Tullus consul consilium publicum habuit an rationem Catilinae habere deberet, si peteret consulatum; nam quaerebatur repetundarum. Catilina ob eam causam destitit a petitione.*[1] It is clear that Cicero and Asconius are referring to the same occasion as Sallust, whose words *post paulo* fix it to the supplementary election in September or October. But there must have been some special reason for this extraordinary and arbitrary action on the part of Volcacius and his senatorial advisers. Sallust gives a reason, itself needing explanation, in the words *quod intra legitimos dies profiteri nequiverit*, the mood of *nequiverit* showing that this was the publicly stated ground. But Sallust evidently thinks that the reason why the *professio* was not accepted was because Catiline was *pecuniarum repetundarum reus*. In this he is clearly wrong. (1) For this would have constituted a technical disqualification, and would have rendered superfluous the act of Volcacius in taking advice. (2) A man was not technically *reus* till after the *nominis delatio* and the constitution of the *iudicium*, and as Catiline's case was still undecided in July 65 (*ad Att.* i, 2), it is inconceivable that the case was set on foot in the autumn of 66. (3) We have the direct

[1] Mommsen (*Staatsr.* i, 485) strangely takes the exclusion to refer to Catiline's candidature in 65, and not 66 at all. But (1) though Catiline might have announced his intention to stand next year, no decision on the part of Volcacius or his advisers could bind the consuls of next year, on whom alone Catiline's exclusion or acceptance would depend. (2) The context in Sallust, as well as a phrase of Dio, ἠτήκει δὲ καὶ αὐτὸς τὴν ἀρχήν, και διὰ τοῦτο ὀργὴν ἐποιεῖτο, (xxxvi, 44) prove that the rejection of his candidature induced Catiline to join the conspiracy at the end of 66 which was to have given him the consulship.

statement of Asconius that the accusation was not brought
by Clodius till 65.[1] The reason must therefore be sought
elsewhere. It is true that Catiline was already the subject
of charges made by the envoys from Africa, and was therefore threatened with an accusation, as implied by Asconius'
words *nam quaerebatur repetundarum.* But the senate's
motive was certainly not pure horror of his conduct in
Africa, for that was by no means uncommon, and even
Cicero, though convinced of his guilt, subsequently thought
of defending him (*ad Att.* i, 2), while Torquatus actually
did so (*pro Sull.* 81). Nor could it have been the mere
result of Catiline's evil reputation, for, though the part
he had played in the Sullan proscriptions was notorious,
this had not stood in his way so far, nor prevented him
from obtaining the praetorship and even the valuable
province of Africa. It was perhaps true that his *primus
in rempublicam aditus equitibus Romanis occidendis fuit*[2]
and his atrocious murder of Marius Gratidianus is well
attested.[3] As to the other crimes perhaps justly attributed
to Catiline, many obviously depended on mere rumour,
had never been judicially investigated and were given
inconsistently by different authorities.[4] Cicero declared,
no doubt, that no crime had been committed in recent
years in which Catiline had not shared, but against this
we must put, for what they are worth, his statements in
pro Coel. 14 foll. He there declares that Catiline was a
mixture of good and evil, and that he himself had at one
time been deceived and regarded him as *bonus civis et*

---

[1] Ascon. 85 : *Torquato et Cotta coss. accusatus est repetundarum
a P. Clodio,* i.e. in 65.

[2] *Q. Cic. de pet. cons.* 2, 9.

[3] *id. ib.* ; Ascon. 84, 87, 90.

[4] Cicero *in tog. cand.* explained by Asconius, gives us some choice
specimens. Sallust and Q. Cicero add to the list. Sallust's
story of an intrigue with a vestal happens to be refuted because
Cicero and his brother had some interest in the lady's reputation
(Sall. c. 15 ; Ascon. 91 ; *de pet. cons.* 2, 9).

optimi cuiusque cupidus.   That Catiline at this point of
his career neither had been nor could have been suspected
of having any dangerous or revolutionary aims of his own
seems practically certain.   It is true that some of the later
writers follow the view of Sallust : *hunc post dominationem
L. Sullae lubido maxima invaserat reipublicae capiundae,
neque id quibus modis adsequeretur, dum sibi regnum
pararet, quicquam pensi habebat* (c. 5).   So Plutarch
(*Cic.* 10 and 11) speaks of a section after Sulla which,
wishing to destroy the present state of things ἰδίων ἕνεκα
πλεονεξιῶν, took Catiline as its κορυφαῖος ; while both
he and Appian (ii, 2) declare that Catiline sought the
consulship with a view to a tyranny.   But there is no
evidence whatever of this long-conceived design, and I will
content myself here with quoting Cicero's statement that
the events of 66 were *aliquanto ante furorem Catilinae et
suspicionem huius coniurationis (pro Sull.* 56).

We have still, therefore, to explain the unusual course
taken by Volcacius, and I am tempted to explain it by the
apparent situation.   It seems probable that, as the year
drew on, Crassus and no doubt Caesar with him, growing
uneasy both at the position of Pompey and the signs of
senatorial activity shown in the persistent attacks on
Cornelius, and the vigorous prosecution of the consuls
designate, favoured and perhaps invited the candidature
of Catiline against the two optimatist candidates, Cotta
and Torquatus, hoping to find in him a useful instrument
for what might have to be done next year.   If this was
the design, and if the senatorial party suspected it, we
have a sufficient explanation of the course taken.   Apart
from technical disabilities such as insufficient age or stand-
ing, or the fact of being *reus* in a criminal suit, the consuls
in accepting candidates had perhaps a certain vague
discretion on personal grounds.   There is no evidence that
this discretion was often used or abused, but the present
case was urgent, Catiline's antecedents were bad, and the
senate had already in a marked way prejudged the latest

charge against him. Volcacius therefore, after fortifying himself with the decision of the *consilium publicum*, on one excuse or another refused during the *legitimi dies* to accept Catiline's *professio*.[1]

The second consular elections in 66, as the result of which Cotta and Torquatus were returned, could hardly have been earlier than October, and the last months of the year would seem to have been unsettled. The accusation of Cornelius had so far proved abortive,[2] but was certain to be renewed, and a similar charge was brought by the *optimates* against Manilius as soon as he laid down the tribuneship on December 10: δίκης τινὸς τῷ Μαλλίῳ πρὸς τῶν δυνατῶν παρασκευασθείσης (D. C. xxxvi, 44). The case, probably only at the stage of *nominis delatio*, seems to have come before Cicero as praetor, and he, willingly or unwillingly, postponed it to the last day of the year (D. C. *loc. cit.* and Plut. *Cic.* 9). Whatever Cicero's original attitude may have been, he promised to defend Manilius when the case came on·next year,[3] and this, like his defence of Cornelius, was regarded by his brother Quintus as a popular act.[4] But the disturbances which

---

[1] The question of the *legitimi dies*, ἐν αἷς ἡμέραις ὑπατείας ἦσαν παραγγελίαι (App. ii, 8), occurs again in connexion with Caesar's first consulship. As it appears from Plut. (*Caes.* 13) that Caesar only reached Rome πρὸς αὐτὰς τὰς ὑπατικὰς ἀρχαιρεσίας, and from Suet. (*Iul.* 18) that it was after the day fixed for the *comitia* had been announced (*edictis comitiis*), the *legitimi dies* were clearly the interval, a *trinundinum*, between the fixture of the date (corresponding to the *promulgatio* of a law) and the election. Mommsen argues that they must have been before the *trinundinum* began, because in 49 Caesar declared *se praesentem trinum nundinum petiturum* (*ad fam.* xvi, 12, 3). But the promise clearly means only that Caesar would make his *professio* at the beginning of the *legitimi dies*, instead of waiting to the last moment.

[2] Ascon. *in Cornel.*, 59 foll.

[3] According to Dio (*loc. cit.*) the promise was extorted by the people; Cicero himself says (in Asconius, 65) that he was urged to the defence by one of the praetors.

[4] *de pet. cons.* 13, 51: where Cicero's claims to popularity lie in *Pompeio ornando, Manili causa recipienda, Cornelio defendendo.*

attended this case on the last day of the year[1] are only important as connected with another affair still more obscure, but undoubtedly of deep political moment.

---

[1] Ascon. 66 : *dicit de disturbato iudicio Maniliano.* That the trial was postponed by Cicero to the last day of the year is clear from Plutarch's words (*Cic.* 9) ἧς ἔτι μόνης κύριος ἦν ἡμέρας στρατηγῶν, ταύτην ἐπίτηδες ὁρίσαι.

II

The Conspiracy of 66–65

IN the middle of December the position of Crassus and Caesar must have been an anxious one. On the one hand was Pompey's almost unbounded power in the East ; on the other was a boom of senatorial vigour, marked by the conviction of Autronius and Sulla, the triumphant election of Cotta and Torquatus, the cavalier treatment of Catiline, and the impending prosecutions of Cornelius and Manilius. If this situation was acquiesced in, the next year might see the popular party driven into a corner. But while the popular leaders were thus probably at a loss, there were certainly several discontented and dissatisfied persons, who in different ways had found their paths and prospects blocked. Autronius and Sulla by the effect of the *lex Calpurnia* were permanently excluded from political life ; a certain Vargunteius was apparently in the same position (*pro Sull.* 6) ; Catiline was outraged at his recent treatment (διὰ τοῦτο ὀργὴν ἐποιεῖτο), and was anticipating a charge of *repetundae*, while there were no doubt many young men of his clique,[1] and especially the able young spendthrift Cn. Piso, ready for any enterprise promising relief or profit. Now from Sallust, Dio Cassius and Cicero we learn that it was these last mentioned persons, all of secondary importance, who in the course of December made a conspiracy to murder the two new consuls and others on the Capitol on January 1.

Sallust (c. 18) after describing the condemnation of Autronius and Sulla, the refusal of Catiline's candidature and the character of Cn. Piso, goes on : *cum hoc Catilina et Autronius circiter Nonas Decembres consilio communicato*

---

[1] We may accept the statements of Sallust (c. 14) and Plutarch (*Cic.* 10) as to the evil influence exercised by Catiline's personality on young men.

parabant in Capitolio kal. Ian. L. Cottam et L. Torquatum consules interficere, ipsi fascibus correptis Pisonem cum exercitu ad occupandas Hispanias mittere. Dio Cassius (xxxvi, 44), after speaking of the charge against Manilius, says that the trial was interrupted by another disturbance :
Πούπλιός τε γὰρ Παῖτος καὶ Κορνήλιος Σύλλας . . . ὕπατοί τε ἀποδειχθέντες καὶ δεκασμοῦ ἁλόντες ἐπεβούλευσαν τοὺς κατηγο-ρήσαντάς σφων Κότταν τε καὶ Τορκουᾶτον . . . ἄλλως τε καὶ ἐπειδὴ αὐτοὶ ἀνθῃρέθησαν, ἀποκτεῖναι· καὶ παρεσκευάσθησαν μεν ἄλλοι τε καὶ Γναῖος Πίσων καὶ Λούκιος Κατιλίνας . . . ᾔτήκει δὲ καὶ αὐτὸς τὴν ἀρχήν καὶ διὰ τοῦτο ὀργὴν ἐποιεῖτο κ. τ. λ.
Cicero (*in tog. cand.*, Ascon. 92) says : *praetereo nefarium illum conatum tuum et paene acerbum . . . reipublicae diem cum, Cn. Pisone socio, ne quem alium nominem, caedem optimatium facere voluisti.*[1]

It appears therefore that, after the murder on January 1, the consulship was to be assumed by Autronius and Catiline,[2] while it was part of the scheme to secure Spain by sending Piso thither with an army. All accounts agree that this plot was discovered, Dio declaring φρουράν τῷ τε Κόττᾳ καὶ τῷ Τορκουάτῳ παρὰ τῆς βουλῆς δοθῆναι. Asconius (92) says that the plot failed because Catiline gave the signal to the conspirators too soon, a cause of failure which Sallust assigns to the second attempt made in February. Putting another statement of Asconius (66) side by side with one of Cicero (*in Cat.* i, 15), I am inclined to discover the failure of the plot in the impatience of Catiline. Asconius believes that Cicero in using the phrase *magnis hominibus auctoribus* in connexion with the *dis-turbatum iudicium Manilianum*, on the last day of the year, was alluding to Catiline and Piso. Cicero says afterwards to Catiline in the senate : ' Do you think that any of us are

[1] Cicero refers to the affair again in *pro Sull.* 68, and adds the name of Vargunteius.

[2] Dio and Suetonius state that Sulla was to have been consul with Autronius, but Sallust and Cicero are better witnesses. Torquatus too, Sulla's later accuser, though this version would have suited his case better, asserted that Sulla had joined the plot *ut Catilinam consulem efficeret* (*pro Sull.* 68).

ignorant *te pridie kal. Ian. Lepido et Tullo coss. stetisse in comitio cum telo? manum consulum et principum civitatis interficiendorum causa paravisse.'* I infer from these two statements that on December 31 Catiline was tempted by the disturbances attending the trial of Manilius to make some premature display of the armed force to be used on the following day, and that, the suspicions of the senate being thus aroused, a bodyguard was decreed for the new consuls, and the outrage on the Capitol in this way prevented.

But there seem to be many mysterious points about this plot of which the facts so far recorded furnish no explanation. If this audacious plan of assassination, got up by a few men, who had already felt the weight of the senatorial hand, was detected, why was nothing done? Dio states that a decree would have been passed against them, εἰ μὴ δήμαρχός τις ἠναντιώθη. Are we to suppose that this tribune was in the plot, or that the senate would have respected any *intercessio* merely intended to save these would-be assassins? It looks far more as if the senate wished to hush the matter up. Cicero implies that the facts of the conspiracy were kept back at the time. It was one *quae facta esse dicitur*, and he at least was not admitted to the confidence of the government. *Patris tui, fortissimi viri atque optimi consulis, scis me consiliis non interfuisse ; scis me, cum mihi summus tecum usus esset, tamen illorum temporum et sermonum expertem fuisse (pro Sull.* 11). Still more extraordinary is the fact that Torquatus the consul himself, within a few months of this plot against his own life, defended Catiline on the charge of *repetundae*, and in reference to this first conspiracy merely remarked *se audisse aliquid, non credidisse (pro Sull.* 81). Nor is the mystery lessened when we find Piso, by all accounts a moving spirit in the affair, actually sent to Spain in accordance with the conspirators' programme, but by the act of the senate.[1] The mere desire to get rid of a dangerous

[1] Sall. c. 19 : *neque tamen senatus provinciam invitus dederat ;* Ascon. 92 : *in Hispaniam missus a senatu.*

and factious young man, suggested by Sallust, Asconius and Dio,[1] is clearly an insufficient explanation, and all the more so because, though only a *quaestor*, he certainly commanded an army in the Hither Province with the title of *pro praetore*.[2] But if the senate's motive in sending Piso to Spain seems inexplicable unless we take into account factors not yet mentioned, it is even less clear why the conspirators, if their aim was mere assassination with a view to regaining the consulship, should have thought of occupying Spain at all. If indeed we could assume that men like Catiline, Autronius and Piso were adopting the rôle of popular leaders, and taking precautions against Pompey's formidable position in the East, we might have an explanation, but for such an assumption there is no evidence and little probability.

At any rate, no official enquiry was made ; no steps were, taken to bring the conspirators to justice ; the affair was studiously hushed up.[3] The suspicion is surely inevitable that there was something behind the facts so far related, something which the *optimates* judged it advisable to ignore and keep back, something which perhaps compromised more important personages, whom it was diplomatic not to provoke. But of course, if this was so, there would be many who knew the facts, and more who suspected them ; and indiscreet allusions to them would not be surprising, especially in after years.

Now we learn from Suetonius that there actually were

---

[1] e.g. Dio says : ἐφοβήθη τε ἡ γερουσία μή τι συνταράξῃ, καὶ εὐθὺς αὐτὸν ἐς Ἰβηρίαν πρόφασιν ὡς καὶ ἐπ, ἀρχήν τινα, ἔπεμψε.

[2] Dessau, 875 : *Cn. Calpurnius Cn. f. Piso quaestor pro pr. ex s. c. provinciam Hispaniam citeriorem optinuit.*

[3] It was no doubt due to this hushing up that the persons to be assassinated are described so differently. Sallust and Dio speak only of the two consuls ; Cicero *in tog. cand.* speaks of *caedem optimatium ;* later (*in Cat.* i, 15) we have *consulum et principum civitatis interficiendorum ;* in *pro Mur.* 38 it has got to be *consilium senatus interficiendi.* The sober phrase of the epitomator *coniuratio de interficiendis consulibus* makes us wish all the more that we had Livy's account.

indiscreet persons who, either in the heat of party strife or the privacy of correspondence, gave utterance to stories which, if true, must have been known or suspected by most public men of the time. From the same source, too, we find that these stories were accepted as true and recorded by at least one contemporary historian of some reputation. It will be best to give the version of Suetonius in full. After narrating the affair of the Transpadani in July 67, he goes on : *nec eo setius maiora mox in urbe molitus est ; siquidem ante paucos dies quam aedilitatem iniret, venit in suspicionem coniurasse cum M. Crasso consulari, item cum P. Sulla et L. Autronio post designationem consulatus ambitus condemnatis, ut principio anni senatum adorirentur, et, trucidatis quos placitum esset, Crassus dictaturam invaderet, ipse ab eo magister equitum diceretur, constitutaque ad arbitrium republica Sullae et Autronio consulatus restitueretur. Meminerunt huius coniurationis Tanusius Geminus in historia, M. Bibulus in edictis, C. Curio pater in orationibus. De hac re significare videtur et Cicero in quadam ad Accium epistula, referens Caesarem in consulatu confirmasse regnum de quo aedilis cogitasset. Tanutius adicit Crassum paenitentia vel metu diem caedi destinatum non obisse, et idcirco ne Caesarem quidem signum quod ab eo dari convenerat dedisse ; convenisse autem Curio ait ut togam de umero deiceret* (Suet. *Iul.* 9).

There seems no reason to doubt that the statements attributed by Suetonius to Bibulus and Curio were actually made. Bibulus in the heat of his conflict with Caesar in 59 may easily have been provoked into saying what he knew or thought he knew ; while Curio was an extreme *optimate* and may well have shown a similar indiscretion perhaps in a published speech. The reference to Cicero cannot be pressed, as no such allusion is found in any extant letter, and also because the phrase *regnum cogitasse* might as well or better refer to the attempt on Egypt in 65. But the citation of Tanusius, a writer of the Caesarian period, used by Plutarch for Caesar's acts in Gaul (*Caes.* 22), shows that Suetonius derived his version from a respectable source. Whether true or not, it proves the existence of suspicions, kept out of sight by Cicero and Sallust, that Crassus and Caesar were at the back of the conspiracy, and that there had been fairly definite rumours afloat as to their aims and plans. As the plans were never carried out, and as no public statement or enquiry was ever made, actual proof was impossible, and even the version, which was allowed to transpire at the time, was equally un-authenticated, and for the same reason.[1] But the version derived from Suetonius seems to suit the political situation, and supplies an intelligible explanation of all that in the other version seems mysterious.

It would appear that Crassus and Caesar, seeing in the coming year senatorial predominance at home, and in-creasing menace from Pompey abroad, took advantage of the useful and unscrupulous instruments which recent disappointments provided, and resolved upon a *coup d'état*. An armed band was to be raised by Catiline, Autronius, Piso, Vargunteius and perhaps Sulla,[2] by which the two new consuls, and no doubt others if they resisted, were to be killed, and the Capitol probably occupied. The attack was to be made when Caesar let his toga fall from his shoulder. Whether Crassus would really have assumed the dictatorship is, of course, uncer-tain, but, in view of the drastic steps to be taken (*republica ad arbitrium constituta*), it is difficult to see what measures short of this would have met the case. During what would perhaps have been only a few days' *dominatio* certain readjustments were to be made. As a precaution against the *optimates*, the conviction of Autronius and

[1] Sallust characteristically tells this story as well as others equally uncertain without any expression of doubt, but, as we have seen, for Cicero it was merely a plot *quae facta esse dicitur* while Asconius (82) introduces the story with : *fuit enim opinio*.

[2] Cicero's defence of Sulla in 62 is far from convincing ; and he was probably in the affair. The omission of Catiline and Piso by Suetonius has little weight against Cicero, Sallust, Asconius and Dio. Piso too is mentioned, but in what Suetonius regards as a second combination.

Sulla, and perhaps the threatened prosecution of Catiline, would probably have been quashed, and the consulship placed in safe hands. As a first *point d'appui* against Pompey, Piso was to command an army in Spain. These steps taken, Crassus could afford to take up his duties as censor, Caesar his humbler post of aedile.

But knowledge or suspicion of the plan reached the senate, perhaps through Catiline's indiscretion on the last day of December, and the popular leaders, knowing of the bodyguard prepared, gave up their design. Crassus stayed at home, and Caesar in some way stopped the *émeute*. There was some anger at the affair in the senate, but Crassus was too powerful to attack, prudent counsels prevailed, and a tribune was found to stop the discussion. No enquiry was made, and the affair was hushed up as far as Crassus and Caesar were concerned. It would seem, indeed, that on one point, viz. the need of taking precautions against Pompey, the senate and the popular leaders were led by this affair to discern their common interest ; for Piso was after all sent to Spain as *quaestor pro praetore* by decree of the senate, but also, as Sallust states, *adnitente Crasso quod eum infestum inimicum Cn. Pompeio cognoverat (Cat.* 19). As to the part taken by the popular leaders in Piso's appointment, Suetonius is in virtual agreement, though he makes it the doing of Caesar rather than of Crassus, and erroneously represents it as a second conspiracy between the former and Piso, with the view of stirring up a revolution, the one from Spain, the other by means of the Transpadani. *Idem Curio sed et M. Actorius Naso auctores sunt conspirasse eum (Caesarem) etiam cum Cn. Pisone . . . cui ob suspicionem urbanae coniurationis provincia Hispania ultro extra ordinem data sit ; pactumque ut simul foris ille, ipse Romae ad res novas consurgerent, per Ambranos et Transpadanos.* Suetonius must have somehow muddled the statements of his authorities,[1] which however, even in this garbled form,

---

[1] Actorius Naso is thought to have been more or less a contemporary of Caesar.

confirm the co-operation of Crassus and Caesar at this time, establish the importance to them of Piso's position in Spain, and give us another hint of the close relation between Caesar and the Transpadani. As to the real motive for Piso's appointment, Sallust's account alone is intelligible.

I am of course far from asserting that the evidence for this obscure conspiracy admits of no interpretation but that which I have given to it, but I claim for my suggestion that, in the light of the general political situation, it gives an intelligible explanation of the few facts established, and of the obvious mystery which surrounded the incident at the time. What Sallust says about Crassus with special reference to the summer of 64 (c. 17) seems to me at least as applicable to 66 and 65. *Fuere ea tempestate qui crederent M. Licinium Crassum non ignarum eius consilii fuisse, quia Cn. Pompeius invisus ipsi magnum exercitum ductabat, cuiusvis opes voluisse contra illius potentiam crescere, simul confisum, si coniuratio valuisset, facile apud illos principem se fore.* The suspicions of such persons were naturally not openly expressed, but I am not sure that Cicero, in the speech made before his own election in 64, did not allow himself to make fairly obvious insinuations. Asconius, at any rate, in commenting on a pretty clear reference to either Crassus or Caesar in connexion with Catiline's candidature in that year, says : *eius quoque coniurationis, quae Cotta et Torquato coss . . . facta est a Catilina et Pisone, arguit M. Crassum auctorem fuisse* (Ascon. 83). Cicero clearly let himself go in this speech, and, though probably he did not mention Crassus by name, we can hardly doubt that he alluded to him with half-veiled insinuation, as he did repeatedly to both Crassus and Caesar in his speeches against Rullus.

The *coup d'état*, if such had been intended, was a failure, and even Piso's despatch to Spain ended in disappointment, since he failed to conciliate the provincials, and met his death, before the year was out, assassinated either by them or by Pompey's friends. What the conspiracy, however,

had done was to usher in a constant and nervous apprehension of plots and cabals. This condition of things was
very marked in 65. It was a year of signs and portents,
and what the soothsayers saw in these was *caedes et incendia
et legum interitus et bellum civile ac domesticum* (*in Cat.*
iii, 30). A new statue of Jupiter was ordered by Cotta
and Torquatus ὅπως αἱ συνωμοσίαι ὑφ' ὧν ἐταράττοντο ἐκφανεῖεν
(D. C. xxxvii, 9). I am inclined to place among these
imaginary conspiracies the design attributed by Sallust
(*loc. cit.*) to Catiline and others in February. When the
original plan was discovered, *in Nonas Feb. consilium
caedis transtulerant; iam tum non consulibus modo sed
plerisque senatoribus perniciem machinabantur*, and if Catiline
had not given the signal too soon, *eo die post conditam
urbem Roman pessimum facinus patratum foret*. It is
surely of all things the least likely that Crassus and Caesar
would have repeated their design after it had once been
discovered, and though Catiline and Autronius might have
persisted, it seems better, in the complete absence of all
other mention of this second and more atrocious plot, to
dismiss it as irresponsible rumour carelessly repeated by
Sallust.

III.

Crassus, Caesar and Catiline to the Elections of 64

WHEN the year 65 began, the popular leaders had still their position both against the senate and against Pompey to secure. Crassus was censor, but though this might be an important position, if things came to a *lectio senatus*, he had no legislative initiative, and he might be hampered by his optimatist colleague Lutatius Catulus. Caesar was aedile, but the popularity gained by his shows and even the impression caused by his restoration of the Marian trophies could only be feelers towards something more decisive. The abandonment of the Manilian prosecution and the ultimate acquittal of Cornelius were so far satisfactory, but the latter, though it might help Cicero later in his rôle of 'popular' candidate, was perhaps more a concession to Pompey, whose quaestor Cornelius had been, than to the *populares*. But Crassus and Caesar did their best both to gain a vantage ground against Pompey and to secure fresh popular support. We learn from Dio Cassius (xxxvii, 9) that Crassus and Catulus were in sharp antagonism over the question of admitting the Transpadani to the full *civitas*. Crassus, however, as censor, could only have enrolled these on the burgess register after their enfranchisement by legislation.[1] Probably, therefore, a tribunician law was to have been proposed, and the dispute between the censors was whether they should or should not give effect to it in the census lists. Obviously no such

---

[1] I have argued this point as against Mommsen's view in *Journ. of Phil.* xxxiii, 65. That Caesar as well as Crassus favoured the Transpadane claim is clear from Suet. *Iul.* 8.

law was passed, and as there are obscure indications in Dio of an Alien Act being passed affecting the Transpadani, we may suppose that senatorial opposition was too strong. But according to Plutarch (*Crass.* 13) there was another δεινὸν πολίτευμα καὶ βίαιον on which Crassus was also opposed by Catulus, viz. the annexation of Egypt. But this no more than the other was a question for the censors to decide. Egypt had been bequeathed to the Roman people in 81, and it was for the senate, or possibly for the people itself, formally to accept the bequest. But, supposing Egypt to be made a province, one of the censors might refuse to give effect to the step by putting obstacles in the way of the usual *locatio* of its *vectigalia*. This is apparently what Catulus did, for Plutarch's expression Αἴγυπτον ποιεῖν ὑποτελῆ Ῥωμαίοις is 'to make Egypt subject to Roman *vectigalia*.' From Suetonius (*Iul.* 11) we find that the prime mover in the affair was Caesar, and that the annexation was to have been the result of a popular law. *Conciliato populi favore temptavit per partem tribunorum ut sibi Aegyptus provincia daretur.* It was therefore to have been declared by law that Egypt was a province and that Caesar should be invested with an extraordinary command in order to annex it. This is what Cicero alludes to when, speaking of the more indirect attempt made in 63, he says : *quod si Alexandria petebatur, cur non eosdem cursus hoc tempore quos L. Cotta L. Torquato coss cucurrerunt?* (*de leg. agrar.* ii, 44). It is impossible to doubt from the evidence that Crassus and Caesar were working closely together and that the possession of Egypt was to have been to them an even stronger bulwark against Pompey than Spain under Piso might have been made. It is, however, equally clear that senatorial and Pompeian influence was as yet too strong, since this attempt, like that to enfranchise the Transpadani, ended in failure.

We now approach the critical consular elections held in 64. Those in 65 call for no particular notice, for they evidently passed off without special excitement (*ad. Att.* i, 1 and 2). Catiline was unable to be a candidate because

the charge of *repetundae* had materialised in the course
of the year, but was still pending in July (*id. ib.*) After
the elections were over, the trial was decided and resulted
in an acquittal contrary to the clearest evidence, and
brought about by the corruption of the jurors and the
praevaricatio of Clodius the accuser. Q. Cicero declares :
*ex eo iudicio tam egens discessit quam quidam iudices eius
ante illud fuerunt* (*de pet. cons.* 3, 10). It has already been
noticed how, with a curious magnanimity, the consul
Torquatus defended the man who was to have been his
assassin. It was known that Catiline, if acquitted, would
be a candidate for the consulship next year, and Cicero
at least can have had no suspicion at this time that he was
meditating any treasonable designs, for he had thought of
defending him, because *spero, si absolutus erit coniunctiorem
illum nobis fore in ratione petitionis* (*ad. Att.* i, 2). That
Cicero did not actually defend Catiline, as Fenestella
declares (Ascon. 85), is abundantly clear. Probably
Catiline knew where more influential support was to be had
than was to be looked for from a *novus homo*, and declined
Cicero's advances.

The year 64 seems to have opened quietly. Caesar and
Crassus had apparently made no further sign since their
failure in the matter of Egypt, though Caesar, now *quaesitor*
in the *quaestio de sicariis*, made evident his Marian
sympathies. Sulla had exempted from the operation of
his law constituting this court the assassins employed by
himself in the proscriptions. But Caesar, disregarding
this, treated these persons, when brought before him, as
ordinary murderers. *In exercenda de sicariis quaestione
eos quoque sicariorum numero habuit qui proscriptione ob
relata civium Romanorum capita pecunias ex aerario
acceperant, quamquam exceptos Corneliis legibus* (Suet.
Iul. 11). It would seem as if the popular leaders were
marking time this year, but concentrating their attention
on the elections, with the view of carrying out a concerted
policy in the following year.

At the outset of the canvassing the *optimates* had clearly

no strong candidate, probably because they had not yet
realised the nature of the combination in preparation.
Both from his letters to Atticus (*ad Att.* i, 1, 2) and from
the long letter of advice addressed to him by his brother
it is clear that Cicero was not counting much at first on
senatorial support, and that he derived most hope from
his connexion with Pompey, the support of the equestrian
order and certain episodes in his career suggestive of
popular sympathies. But it gradually transpired that
Catiline was deliberately working with another candidate,
C. Antonius, a man of hardly better reputation than his
own, who had been expelled from the senate in 70, but, like
many others, had recovered his rank with the praetorship
(Plut. *Cic.* 17). Not only was it known that these two
men of dangerous antecedents had combined forces for
the elections, but it was more than suspected that they
were both being supported by Crassus and Caesar.
Asconius can hardly be wrong in detecting a reference to
one of the popular leaders in a statement made by Cicero
shortly before the elections : *dico, patres conscripti,
superiore nocte cuiusdam hominis nobilis et valde in hoc
largitionis quaestu noti et cogniti domum Catilinam et
Antonium cum sequestribus suis convenisse.*[1] The probabilities are strongly in favour of Asconius' own statement :
coierunt enim ambo (Catiline and Antonius) *ut Ciceronem
consulatu deicerent, auditoribus usi firmissimis M. Crasso
et C. Caesare.* That Sallust alludes to the suspicions of
Crassus' connexion with Catiline at this point of time we
have already noticed, though, in accordance with his whole
presentation, the supposed connexion is not so much
electoral support as complicity in a revolutionary conspiracy (Sall. c. 16). In accordance with this view, Sallust
thus describes Catiline's position and aims in 64 : *his
amicis sociisque confisus Catilina, simul quod aes alienum
per omnes terras ingens erat, et quod plerique Sullani milites,
largius suo usi, rapinarum et victoriae veteris memores
civile bellum exoptabant, opprimendae reipublicae consilium*

[1] Quoted in Ascon. 83.

cepit.[1] Plutarch, probably following Sallust, gives a similar account of the situation, though he goes so far as to declare that Etruria and most of Cisalpine Gaul were already roused to revolt.[2] According to Sallust it was in the beginning of June that Catiline called a meeting of his chief supporters, including already Lentulus Sura, Cassius Longinus, Autronius, Cethegus and the rest whose names figure so prominently at the close of 63. In addition to the men actually assembled, Sallust darkly hints at others *occultius huiusce consilii participes*, induced by *dominationis spes*.[3] At any rate, what Catiline had to lay before them was not the programme of a consulship, but *praemia coniurationis*, though Sallust makes him conclude with the words: *haec ego, ut spero, vobiscum una consul agam*. But his friends not being contented with vague promises, *pollicetur novas tabulas, proscriptionem locupletium, magistratus, sacerdotia, rapinas*, and the other things which war brings and victors desire. He concludes with the declaration *esse in Hispania citeriore Pisonem, in Mauretania P. Sittium cum exercitu, consilii sui participes; petere consulatum C. Antonium, quem collegam sibi fore speraret.*

Now it seems quite impossible to accept such a *coniuratio* with such a programme as existing or even thought of in the summer of 64. It is no doubt true that intrigues were in the air, of which all suspected the existence, but no one knew the character. Cicero was justified in saying, 16

---

[1] Sall. c. 17; the situation assigned by Sallust to the period before the elections in 64 fairly corresponds with that after the elections of 63.

[2] Plut. *Cic.* 10 : ἐπῆρτο δ' ἡ Τυρρηνία πρὸς ἀπόστασιν ὅλη καὶ τὰ πολλὰ τῆς ἐντὸς Ἄλπεων Γαλατίας.

[3] Sallust can hardly be intentionally referring to Caesar and Crassus. He is more probably reflecting the suspicion of the time that powerful men were behind, and perhaps confusing this with the known support received by Catiline in his candidature in 64. Cicero (*in Cat.* ii, 19) speaks equally vaguely of a class of men, *qui, quamquam aere alieno premuntur, tamen dominationem expectant, rerum potiri volunt.* I take this, however, as intended for a covert allusion to Caesar. Sallust may conceivably be alluding to Crassus alone, whom he takes little trouble to defend.

months later, *iam diu . . . in his periculis coniura-*
tionis insidiisque versamur (*in Cat.* i, 31) just as he alludes
both in *de leg. agr.* and in *pro Rab.* (*de leg. agr.* i, 9, 26 ;
pro Rab. 12, 33) to plots and intrigues emanating from
traitors and revolutionaries. But these expressions do
not imply more than the nervous suspense and mistrust
naturally left behind by the mysterious affair of 66. If
Sallust were correct, we should have to suppose, not only
that Catiline was organising this conspiracy during the
first half of 64, for which there is no evidence, but that,
having made ready to strike in June or July, he allowed
all his preparations to be held up for more than a year.
But outside Sallust and Plutarch there is no indication
of any revolutionary or anti-social conspiracy at this time,
far less of any threatened revolt in Italy. On the other
hand, according to Sallust, not only the existence, but
some of the details of this conspiracy were so far common
knowledge at the time, that they were the cause of Cicero's
election to the consulship. We are told that Curius, one
of the conspirators, blabbed to his mistress Fulvia, and
that she, *tale periculum reipublicae haud occultum habuit,*
sed . . . de Catilinae coniuratione . . . compluribus narravit.
That circumstance, says Sallust, *imprimis studia hominum*
accendit ad consulatum mandandum M. Tullio Ciceroni.[1]
That by *hominum* is meant especially the governing or
senatorial class, is shown by the following sentence :
' for till then most of the nobles were jealous of " new
men," and thought the consulship degraded by their
election.'

Now it will appear on examination that this version is
not only unsupported by other evidence, but is incon-
gruous with the general situation, as well as full of inner
inconsistencies and improbabilities. In the first place,
if the candidature of Catiline was supported by Crassus
and Caesar, as Asconius asserts, and as Cicero himself
seems to have believed, we must suppose one of two things.

[1] Sall. c. 23 ; Appian (ii, 3) tells the same story about Curius
and Fulvia, but not in connexion with the elections in 64.

On the supposition that the popular leaders knew of this revolutionary and anti-social plot, being prepared by their nominee, it is clear that they were virtually the real heads of the conspiracy, and that the promises made by Catiline were indirectly authorized by them.   The mere statement of this suggestion explodes it, for if there was one man in the state whose interests were diametrically opposed to such a programme, it was surely Crassus.   Nor can any act be attributed to Caesar during his whole career which favours the view that he would have countenanced such designs. On the other supposition, the plot must have been kept secret from Crassus and Caesar, and Catiline and Antonius, while receiving support from the popular leaders, were throwing dust in their eyes, and working for ends purely their own.   We should then have to believe that, while Fulvia was spreading her information broadcast, and while the nobles were actually giving up their prejudices against ' new men ' through their belief in the plot, the two most long-sighted men in Rome knew nothing of it.

If on the other hand we discard Asconius, and refuse to believe that Catiline had any backers in his candidature, then what were Crassus and Caesar doing at this critical juncture ?   They were certainly active and alert in 65, and Caesar at least was playing a calculated game in the beginning of 63, but in 64 they were letting everything drift.

But the details of Sallust's story will not hold water. Even if the indiscreet gossip of Fulvia (*compluribus narravit*) was responsible for Cicero's election, it is inconceivable that such a leakage of his plans would have gone on unnoticed by Catiline for seventeen months, and yet we find Fulvia still giving information in November 63. Again, if Lentulus, Cethegus and the rest were definitely members of a sworn conspiracy in June 64, what were they doing till we next hear of them more than a year later ? Would men like Cethegus or the rest, needing immediate relief from debt, have acquiesced in such indefinite postponement of relief ?   Nor is it easy to understand how

Cassius Longinus, as we know from Q. Cicero (*de pet. cons.* 7), a candidate for the consulship, could have joined a conspiracy avowedly counting on the election of Catiline and Antonius.   That Sallust is not very exact as to dates is indicated by Catiline's supposed reference to Piso as an ally in Spain, for Piso, as we learn from Asconius (93), had been killed in the previous year : *Piso autem, cum haec dicerentur* (just before the elections in 64) *perierat*.   As for Sittius in Mauretania, the assertion that he had an army there, or was a party to the conspiracy, is sufficiently disposed of by Cicero (*pro Sull.* 56 to 59).

With regard to other evidence, the argument against Sallust is mainly *e silentio*.   It is certain that Q. Cicero knew nothing of any conspiracy when he wrote the *de pet. cons.*, for in his enumeration of points to Catiline's dis-advantage (*de pet. cons.*, 2, 9 foll.) he would never have omitted this weightiest charge of all, if he had known of it.   Cicero's own speech *in toga candida* is, of course, not fully available, but in one extant passage he declares that Catiline's candidature is an outrage against *principes civitatis*, senators, *equites* and people (in Ascon. 89) ; but the reasons assigned are all taken from the past, and Asconius is clearly aware of no conspiracy at this time. The impression conveyed to my mind is that Sallust has deliberately antedated the existence of a conspiracy against the established order, has brought Catiline a year too soon into close connexion with the desperadoes of October and November 63, and in order to explain Cicero's election, has prematurely introduced Curius and Fulvia upon the scene.   I cannot doubt that his motive was to exonerate Caesar from all suspicion of complicity with what happened in the second half of 63.   If that conspiracy was merely the culmination of a long-cherished *consilium reipublicae capiundae*, conceived by Catiline almost from his first entrance into public life, what reason could there be for suspecting Caesar, or for bringing him into the narrative at all ?   Of Crassus' reputation he is not quite so careful, for he mentions the suspicions against him and their ground without troubling himself to discredit them. It is strange that he should not have realised that suspicion of Crassus involved suspicion of Caesar, for the two were known to be working together at this time. Indeed Sallust's extreme reticence about Caesar must be regarded as highly suspicious. In connexion with the affair of 66 it is intelligible, because there had been a general disposition to hush it up; but to eliminate Caesar and Crassus from all interest in the elections in 64 is not only to excite speculation as to what their position was, but to ignore the common knowledge as to Catiline's backers which clearly descended to Asconius.

I take that as the key to the situation. Caesar and Crassus, having failed throughout 65, were determined to have a strong and unscrupulous executive at their back in 63. Catiline and Antonius were to be consuls, and by their agency and the support of some equally dependable tribunes the republic was still to be in effect *ad arbitrium constituta*. At what precise point the *optimates* became aware of this combination we do not know, but it could not wholly escape notice, and, in view of events in 66, it was bound to cause alarm. We may be sure that Catiline made no promises of *novae tabulae*, but he was for the time a ruined man, and he had many ruined friends, and who knows that there was not some indiscreet and irresponsible talk. There was certainly no attempt to rouse Etruria or Gaul to revolt, but Catiline may have canvassed the discontented Sullan colonists, just as Cicero himself announced his intention of canvassing Gaul (*ad Att.* i, 1, 2). Autronius and the rest were not yet members of a sworn conspiracy, but some of them may well have been among the *sequestres* spoken of by Cicero. It was not the disclosures of Fulvia, but the realisation of this new combination on the part of the popular leaders, which induced the *optimates* to abandon their prejudices against new men, and to give their support to Cicero.

It is certain that the elections were marked by unusual violence and bribery. The senate had to reinforce by special decree a *lex Fabia* limiting the number of *sectatores* accompanying the candidates.[1] It further prepared to pass a decree in favour of a new bribery law more severe than the *lex Calpurnia*. This, however, was vetoed by Q. Mucius, one of the tribunes, who, according to Cicero, was bought by his opponents : *quam ob rem augete* . . *mercedem Q. Muci ut perseveret legem impedire, ut coepit senatus consultum ; sed ego ea lege contentus sum,* etc. (the *lex Calpurnia*, quoted by Ascon. 88 ; conf. 83). It was apparently in the debate on this law that Cicero delivered the speech *in toga candida*. It is not likely, however, that the bribery was all on one side, and at any rate the combination of the *optimates* with the equestrian order was strong enough to carry Cicero to the head of the poll, Antonius being elected over the head of Catiline by only a few centuries.[2]

[1] *pro Mur.* 34, 71 : *Itaque et legi Fabiae quae est de numero sectatorum et senatus consulto quod est L. Caesare cos.* (i.e. 64) *factum restiterunt.*

[2] Ascon 94 ; Sall. *Cat.* 24 ; Plut. *Cic.* 11 : ταῦτα δὴ (the union of Catiline and Antonius) τῶν καλῶν καὶ ἀγαθῶν οἱ πλεῖστοι προαισ- θόμενοι τὸν Κικέρωνα προσῆγον ἐπὶ τὴν ὑπατείαν.

IV

Caesar and Crassus between the Elections of 64 and 63

A S a result of the elections, the plans of the popular leaders were deranged. It was true that Antonius would be consul next year, but he was a man of no political ability, and unfitted to carry through a revolutionary programme. It would seem, however, that the tribunician elections were more favourable, and this circumstance might suggest certain readjustments later in the year. As to the immediate effect of his defeat on Catiline, we have no very clear information. Sallust indeed, after recording the election, says at once (c. 25) : *neque tamen Catilinae furor minuebatur, sed in dies plura agitare, arma per Italiam locis opportunis parare, pecuniam sua aut amicorum fide sumptam mutuam Faesulas ad Manlium . . . portare.* At the same time Catiline is represented as intriguing with men of every class, and especially with clever but dissolute women, through whom he hoped *servitia sollicitare, urbem incendere,* and so to win over or murder their husbands. As Sallust goes on at once to the consular elections in 63, this being his sole reference to what happened in the intervening 12 months, it is not clear whether he assigns these acts to the last half of 64 or to the first half of 63 or to both. At any rate this account of a reorganised conspiracy, including now the burning of the city, receives no confirmation from any other source, even Plutarch, except in the matter of a long-designed plan, using in what follows better authority than Sallust's perhaps careless or imperfect memory.

What we may regard as certain is that from the date of Cicero's election he had in Catiline a bitter and unscrupulous enemy. From what is left of the speech *in toga candida,* delivered a few days before the elections, we cannot wonder at this. For Cicero seems to have collected all the foulest personal charges against Catiline, and for that matter against Antonius too, and to have thrown in his teeth the butcheries of the proscriptions, the corruption in Africa, of which he had been acquitted, and complicity in the attempted murder of the consuls in 66. Catiline's was not a forgiving character, and we can well believe that he repeatedly made attempts on Cicero's life both as *consul designatus* and as *consul*.[1]

But this is far from implying the existence of a regular conspiracy such as Sallust describes. As a matter of fact, the one certain glimpse we get of Catiline at this time shows him to have been on the defensive, for by an extremely dexterous stroke Lucceius in the last half of 64 accused him of murder in the Sullan proscriptions. *Post effecta enim comitia consularia et Catilinae repulsam fecit eum inter sicarios L. Lucceius* (Ascon. 91). As Caesar, the *quaesitor* of this court, had himself set the example of disregarding Sulla's exempting clause, and as Catiline's guilt was notorious, Caesar must have been put in an embarrassing position. He was, however, equal to the occasion, for ὁ Κατιλείνας ἐπὶ τοῖς αὐτοῖς ἐκείνοις αἰτίαν (πολλοὺς γὰρ καὶ αὐτὸς τῶν ὁμοίων ἀπεκτόνει) λαβὼν ἀπελύθη (Dio Cass. xxxvii, 10). The incident seems to me important as proving beyond a doubt Caesar's interest in Catiline, and, as the affair was *post effecta comitia consularia*, making it at least probable that Catiline would have the support of the popular leaders in his next candidature.

Whatever then may have been the secret designs of Catiline, we cannot accept the overt acts attributed to him at this time by Sallust. On the contrary, as far as the evidence goes, Catiline would seem to have been inactive during the later months of 64 and the earlier months of 63. Plutarch's account of the situation at this point seems true, though perhaps not the whole truth : καὶ τὰ μὲν περὶ

---

[1] in Cat. i, 15 : *ac iam illa omitto* . . . *quotiens tu me designatum, quotiens consulem interficere conatus es.* Conf. ib. 11 : *quam diu mihi consuli designato insidiatus es.*

Κατιλείναν ἔμελλεν ἔτι, τοὺς πολλοὺς λάνθανοντα (*Cic.* 12). But there are signs that the popular leaders were readjusting their programme. They had after all one consul in their interest and several at least of the tribunes. No doubt Catiline would have been a far more efficient agent, but something might be done even with inferior tools. Accordingly we find from Dio Cassius (xxxvii, 25) that a comprehensive legislative programme was prepared by some of the new tribunes and Antonius. οἱ γὰρ δήμαρχοι τὸν Ἀντώνιον τὸν ὕπατον . . . προσλαβόντες, ὁ μέν τις τοὺς παῖδας τῶν ὑπὸ τοῦ Σύλλου ἐκπεσόντων πρὸς τὰς ἀρχὰς ἦγεν, ὁ δὲ τῷ τε Παίτῳ . . . καὶ τῷ Σύλλα . . . τῷ μετ' αὐτοῦ ἁλόντι τό τε βουλεύειν καὶ τὸ ἄρχειν ἐξεῖναι ἐδίδου, ἄλλος χρεῶν ἀποκοπάς, ἄλλος κληρουχίας καὶ ἐν τῇ Ἰταλίᾳ καὶ ἐν τῷ ὑπηκόῳ γενέσθαι ἐσηγεῖτο. Now Dio shows himself on the whole well informed as to the events of 63, and his association of Antonius with the tribunes not only corresponds with the probabilities of the situation, but is confirmed by Plutarch, as far at least as the agrarian law is concerned. Διὸ καὶ τῷ νόμῳ προσεῖχον ἄλλοι τε τῶν ἐπιφανῶν καὶ πρῶτος Ἀντώνιος . . . ὡς τῶν δέκα γενησόμενος (*Cic.* 12).

Of these legislative proposals mentioned by Dio only one is unconfirmed by other authorities, viz. that for the abolition of debts.[1]   If the Greek historian is not mistaken about this, it must have been proposed by some independent tribune, perhaps with secret encouragement from Antonius, whose own debts were heavy. The other measures were no doubt parts of the new popular programme, and had nothing whatever to do with Catiline, though Plutarch regarded them as προαγῶνες of his conspiracy. The proposal to restore their political rights to the sons of the Marian exiles is confirmed by Cicero, who in his list of

---

[1] Cicero, however, in two passages uses language which might imply that he had defeated such a law. In *ad Att.* ii, 1, 11 he speaks of himself as *vindicem aeris alieni*; and in *ad fam.* v, 6, 8 he says that he *ex obsidione feneratores exemerit*. These expressions, however, might refer to the conspiracy of Catiline after the elections in 63; cf. also his remarks on debt in *de Officiis* ii, 24, 84.

consular speeches (*ad Att.* v. 1, 3) mentions one *de proscriptorum filiis*. Cicero probably opposed it as likely to threaten the whole position of the *Sullani homines*, an eventuality which, as far as the land question was concerned, was guarded against by the agrarian law. From *pro Sull.* 64 we know that the proposal to relieve Autronius and Sulla from the effects of the *lex Calpurnia* was made by L. Caecilius, a half-brother of the latter. If Dio's version of it is correct, its object can hardly have been other than to allow Autronius to stand with Catiline for the consular elections in the summer. If we are to believe Cicero's special pleading for Sulla (*loc. cit.*), the law was not to reverse the verdict of the *quaestio de ambitu*, but to substitute the milder penalties of the earlier law for those of the *lex Calpurnia*. As this would have been quite as revolutionary an interference with legal procedure, and less satisfactory to all parties concerned, I am sceptical of Cicero's version, and inclined to prefer Dio's. Cicero asserts that Caecilius withdrew the bill at Sulla's request, but, as other interests than Sulla's were clearly involved, it was probably let fall with the acquiescence of the popular leaders as too flagrant a violation of judical forms. But the agrarian law, imperfectly described by Dio, was the really important item of the programme. Plutarch (*loc. cit.*) says that by this law the tribunes were δεκαδαρχίαν καθιστάντες αὐτοκρατόρων ἀνδρῶν, οἷς ἐφεῖτο πάσης μὲν Ἰταλίας πάσης δὲ Συρίας καὶ ὅσα διὰ Πομπηίου νεωστὶ προσώριστο κυρίους ὄντας πωλεῖν τὰ δημόσια . . . συνοικίζειν πόλεις, χρήματα λαμβάνειν ἐκ τοῦ ταμιείου. This was of course the law proposed for Caesar by Servilius Rullus and criticised by Cicero in the three extant speeches *de lege agraria*. The main object of the law as agrarian was the foundation of colonies in Italy, at once for the *plebs urbana* on the *ager Campanus* and any other remaining public land, in the near future for other persons, as occasion might offer, on Italian land to be purchased by the state. The immediate scheme for the colonisation of Capua was suited to a popular programme; the working out of the

more remote scheme involved at once a commanding
position in the empire for the popular leaders and their
supporters, and might, when the time came, serve as a
basis of negotiation with Pompey and render possible the
offer of land for his soldiers. To provide money for the
scheme, a huge agrarian fund was to be formed, partly
by selling public domain lands in several provinces, partly
by appropriating the *vectigalia* from the new provinces
in the East, and especially by treating Egypt and its
vectigalia as belonging to the empire in accordance with
the testament of its late king. Not only the collection
and management of this fund, but the whole task of
purchase and colonisation were to be in the hands of ten
commissioners with extraordinary judicial, executive, and,
if necessary, military powers for five years. The scheme
was one of extraordinary audacity and astuteness, for
Caesar and Crassus, who of course would have been among
the ten, would not only have had a new financial system
at their disposal, but would have found themselves the
virtual masters of Egypt, the strategical *point d'appui*
against Pompey, which they had vainly sought to gain
in 65.[1]

But the popular leaders, who from reasons partly but
perhaps not wholly explained by their delicate relations
with Pompey, were all this time keeping themselves in the
background, now experienced the full disadvantage of
having no better instruments to work with than obscure
tribunes.

The advocacy of Rullus, a mere man of straw, had no
chance against the practised pleading of Cicero, who
represented the whole scheme as nothing but an attempt to
set up a *decemvirale regnum*, directed alike against Pompey,

[1] For a fuller consideration of the Caesarian policy underlying
the Rullan proposal I venture to refer to an article on the subject
in the *Journal of Philology*, xxxii, 64. Besides dexterously and
far-sightedly meeting the situation as against Pompey, the measure
was a real agrarian law, and not a mere pretence of one, as Cicero
asserted. All the principles of Caesar's later agrarian legislation
may be traced in this abortive scheme.

the interests of the people and the solvency of the empire. The measure was probably withdrawn without being proposed, though Plutarch (*Cic.* 12) states that Cicero, after having opposed the bill in the senate, proceeded to the comitia, defeated the law and so discomfited the tribunes ὥστε μηδὲν ἀντιλέγειν. As the other tribunician measures were also defeated by Cicero's agency (D. C. xxxvii, 25), the year began in mortification and perhaps embarrassment for Caesar and Crassus, and the *optimates* no doubt began to congratulate themselves on their new champion.

Now if the situation up to this point had been anything like what I have suggested, it is impossible to suppose that Caesar and Crassus would accept this defeat, or desist from further attempts to establish their own position and that of the popular party against the senatorial obstructionists in the present, and the possible action of Pompey in the future.

As we view the situation, it appears that there were only three courses open : to continue the attempt to secure adequate executive agents at the elections, to repeat at a favourable opportunity the design of a *coup d'état*, or by some means to arrive at a *modus vivendi* with Pompey.

I think it well to repeat here that, with the exception of Sallust's statements in *cc.* 23-25, already discussed, and Plutarch's vaguer repetition, we have no evidence whatever of any definite conspiracy being formed by Catiline up to this point either inside or outside Rome. Cicero's vague and nervous allusions to domestic and intestine dangers do not imply any such conspiracy, nor do any attempts made at this time by Catiline on Cicero's life, for these were the natural results of bitter personal enmity, and were met, as Cicero expressly says, *non publico praesidio sed diligentia privata* (*in Cat.* i, 11). It is necessary, therefore, to reject not only the story already discussed of Fulvia's revelations in the summer of 64, but also Sallust's further statement (c. 26) : *namque a principio consulatus sui multa pollicendo per Fulviam effecerat ut Q. Curius . . .*

consilia Catilinae sibi proderet.[1] Sallust says of Catiline at this time : *neque interea quietus erat, sed omnibus modis Ciceroni insidias parabat,* and this we may accept as meaning that he was engrossed for the present on plans of personal revenge.

It may be presumed that during the earlier part of 63 the first of the three alternative courses suggested above was the one contemplated by the popular leaders. Catiline had certainly again announced himself as a candidate for the consulship, and, though there is no direct evidence that he was still supported by Caesar or Crassus, I argue that he must have been, unless we suppose that, after their repeated but futile efforts in the last few years, they were prepared to leave the elections in this critical year to chance. They seem, it is true, after the withdrawal of the Caecilian proposal, to have had no second candidate in view, but as there was no second Cicero among the other aspirants, this was perhaps less vital than to have one representative prepared to go all lengths. But they must have realised that it might be necessary to go all lengths, or that a man like Catiline, if unsuccessful or desperate, might decide to go all lengths in his own way.   It seems to me that we do the author of the Rullan law much less than justice unless we suppose him far-sighted enough to realise the possibilities of serious disturbance before the year was out. Such disturbances might easily compromise the popular party, and, especially with a consul like Cicero, might play into the hands of the senatorial government. The *senatus consultum ultimum*, the legal validity of which, after the acquittal of Opimius, it was useless to question, was a formidable weapon, and by its means, even with a tactless and inexperienced politician like Marius, the senate had almost annihilated the popular party in the year 100.   It

---

[1] If, as stated by Sallust and Appian, Fulvia's suspicions were first aroused by the boasts of Curius about his coming good fortune, the incident must belong to the period of a fully formed plot with revolutionary designs, and that, as we shall see, was after the elections in 63.

is in the light of these considerations, as it seems to me, that we must explain the extraordinary impeachment of Rabirius undertaken under Caesar's instructions by Labienus, one of the tribunes, in the spring of this year. Its object was not to contest the senate's right to pass the decree, or the consul's right to give effect to it as conditioned by precedent. It was intended to press both on senate and people the heavy responsibility involved in its application, and the likelihood of grave and unjustifiable incidents following in its train. An incident of the kind had occurred 37 years before, when, after the passing of the last decree, Rabirius was said to have killed Saturninus. The deed was supposed to be covered by the senate's decree and the consequent action of Marius. But it was now alleged that Saturninus had been a prisoner at the time, with his safety guaranteed by the consul, so that Rabirius had acted not under the consul, but against his orders. To reveal the possibility of such a murder under the supposed sanction of the last decree must have been the object of Caesar's manœuvre, and there can be little doubt that the condemnation of Rabirius would have seriously embarrassed the government in the event of prompt and drastic action being called for by disturbances later in the year. But Caesar made the mistake of reviving, with a view to impress the public imagination, the obsolete and awe-inspiring procedure of kingly times, and this gave Cicero his second chance of virtually defeating what was in itself a dexterous stroke of policy.[1] It was a defeat, however, which would hardly affect the issue of the main campaign, and the position was more than restored when Labienus renewed the *lex Domitia* on priestly elections, and, in consequence, Caesar was triumphantly appointed *pontifex maximus* (D. C. xxxvii, 37).[2]

[1] I have worked out this view of the impeachment in an article ' On the political and legal aspects of the trial of Rabirius ' in the *Journal of Philology*, xxxiv, 67.

[2] Dio narrates this after the collapse of the final conspiracy. But Labienus went out of office on December 10, and Caesar's election was certainly in the first half of the year.

V

The Consular Elections of 63

O F the events connected with the consular elections we get our best account from Cicero in the *pro. Murena*, delivered in the course of November. Plutarch, however, and Dio Cassius both give useful details. Catiline was opposed by three optimatist candidates, Silanus, Murena and Servius Sulpicius, and it is clear that he conducted his canvass by violent and unscrupulous methods. But there is nothing to show that he was the head of an organised *coniuratio*, like that depicted by Sallust for a year earlier, or like that which we shall find in existence at the end of the year.

Catiline was undoubtedly looking for support to discontented classes in the state, both in Rome and Italy. The country voters, as Cicero had realised in his own canvass, might have great weight, and of these there was a considerable section which might be won over by specious and reckless promises. These were the Sullan colonists on the one hand, whose extravagance and bad farming had brought them to ruin, and on the other many of the Italian farmers whom these soldiers had dispossessed. Both classes were especially numerous in Etruria, where the *plebs* was *egestate simul et dolore iniuriae novarum rerum cupida, quod Sullae dominatione agros bonaque omnia amiserant*, and where there were many *ex Sullanis coloniis, quibus lubido atque luxuria ex magnis rapinis nihil reliqui fecerat* (Sall. c. 28). In Rome too there were many old soldiers, who had already got rid of their land, and who, together with miscellaneous classes of men under a cloud, especially the cloud of debt, might be expected to support a ' popular ' candidate, and all the more if he dexterously held out hopes of relief suited to their several cases.

That Catiline had already at this point sent arms to

Etruria, or prepared for a revolt, is not supported by any evidence except that of Sallust and Plutarch; but nothing is more likely from what we know of the man and the situation than that his promises went far beyond what Crassus or Caesar would have sanctioned. There may even already have been irresponsible talk about the alleviation of debt or the possibility of proscriptions. Catiline was a dangerous instrument to use, difficult to control and not unlikely to produce serious complications for his employers, which might even eventually induce them to throw him over.

We are told by Plutarch (c. 14) that Catiline received much encouragement from Sulla's old soldiers, especially those ταῖς Τυρρηνικαῖς ἐγκατεσπαρμένοι πόλεσιν, and that some of them, headed by Manlius, παρῆσαν εἰς Ῥώμην συναρχαιρεσιάσοντες. This is confirmed and explained by Cicero himself, who speaks of Catiline in his canvass as *alacrem atque laetum, stipatum choro inventutis, vallatum indicibus atque sicariis, inflatum cum spe militum tum conlegae mei, quemadmodum dicebat ipse, promissis, circumfluentem colonorum Arretinorum et Faesulanorum exercitu, quam turbam dissimillimo ex genere distinguebant homines perculsi Sullani temporis calamitate.*[1] We can readily understand the alarm of the *optimates,* and their desperate efforts to defeat a candidate adopting such disorderly and threatening methods, and suspected of having still more influential supporters in the background. Every attempt was made to frighten the people *ne Catilina consul fieret,* and owing to suspicions, which can hardly be misunderstood, a new law against *ambitus* was hurried forward.

The law was carried on the proposal of Cicero as a *lex Tullia,* but according to his own assertion the suggestion came from Servius Sulpicius, one of the senatorial candidates, who would have inserted certain drastic clauses, which the consul contrived to eliminate. Dio Cassius

[1] The passage in the *pro Murena,* from which my quotations are taken, is 23, 26 to 46, 53.

correctly enough gives the main point of the law, though additional details may be gathered from statements of Cicero. Ἔδοξε τῇ βουλῇ . . . δέκα ἐτῶν φυγήν . . . τοῖς ἐπιτιμίοις τοῖς ἐπὶ τῷ δεκασμῷ τεταγμένοις προσνομοθετῆσαι (D. C. xxxvii, 29). It appears from Cicero that Crassus spoke in the discussion on this law, but whether in general support of it, or in support of Cicero's objections to certain extreme suggestions of Sulpicius, it is impossible to decide.

Remembering Cicero's bitter invective against Catiline on the occasion of a similar proposal in the previous year, and the blocking of the measure by a tribune, we may be surprised at the comparative smoothness with which the *lex Tullia* went through, and perhaps even be inclined to wonder whether at the last moment the popular leaders had any thought of dissociating themselves from their compromising agent. There were, however, sharp passages of arms in the debate, and one of them is recorded by Cicero when he alludes to Catiline's rejoinder to Cato : *si quod esset in suas fortunas incendium excitatum, id se non aqua sed ruina exstincturum.*[1] The passing of the law had the effect of increasing Catiline's violence, and, according to Cicero, he indulged in open threats against the republic (*reipublicae minitabatur*). That, however, was only the consul's interpretation of Catiline's reported declaration in a *contio* that no loyal defender of the unfortunate could be found, who was not himself an unfortunate ; *et minime timidum et valde calamitosum esse oportere eum qui esset futurus dux et signifer calamitosorum.* These vague words, uttered on the day before that fixed for the elections, were, according to Cicero, the reason why *factum est senatus consultum referente me ne postero die comitia haberentur, ut de his rebus in senatu agere possemus.* It is however probable, and the suggestion seems confirmed by Plutarch and Dio Cassius, that Cicero's real reason for having the elections postponed was information received by him of a

---

[1] Sallust (c. 31) makes Catiline say this at a later stage, after Cicero's first speech : *quoniam . . . praeceps agor, incendium meum ruina exstinguam.*

plot against his own life, to be carried out amid the confusion of the elections. According to Plutarch (c. 14)
Catiline was βεβουλευμένος ἀνελεῖν τὸν Κικέρωνα περὶ αὐτὸν τῶν
ἀρχαιρεσιῶν θόρυβον, but Cicero, the proofs not being quite
conclusive, τὴν ἡμέραν τῶν ἀρχαιρεσιῶν ὑπερθέμενος . . . ἐκάλει
τὸν Κατιλείναν εἰς τὴν σύγκλητον, καὶ περὶ τῶν λεγομένων ἀνέκρινεν.
Dio agrees as to the day fixed for the assassination, which
failed because ὁ Κικέρων προμαθὼν τὸ ἐπιβούλευμα τῇ τε
γερουσίᾳ ἐμήνυσεν αὐτὸ καὶ κατηγορίαν αὐτοῦ πολλὴν ἐποιήσατο
(xxxvii, 29).   We may take it, however, from Cicero
himself that, when the senate met again on the day which
had been fixed for the *comitia*, he did not tax Catiline
with the plot against himself, but merely asked for an
explanation of the speech in the *contio*. Catiline, so far
from excusing himself, declared that of two bodies in the
state, one decrepit with a feeble head, the other vigorous
but without a head, the latter should lack a head no longer.[1]
The senate groaned, but, though Cicero says not very convincingly that Catiline ought never to have left the house
alive, no further action was taken.

What seems perfectly clear is that up to the eve of the
elections Cicero, though evidently nervous, had no knowledge of a conspiracy against the state, and that, even with
regard to the plot against himself, he had not sufficient
evidence to lay before the senate.   That body had decreed
the postponement of the elections under the impression
that the consul had grave matters to communicate, but
the next day's meeting, with Cicero's statement and
Catiline's reply, left it sceptical and unconvinced. Not
only does Dio Cassius say : οὐκ ἔπεισέ σφας ψηφίσασθαί τι
ὧν ἠξίου, οὔτε γὰρ πιθανὰ ἐξηγγελκέναι κ. τ. λ (c. 29), but Cicero
himself declares in his speech of Nov. 8 that too many
senators *spem Catilinae mollibus sententiis aluerunt, coniurationem nascentem non credendo corroboraverunt* (*in Cat.* i,
30).

[1] Plutarch (c. 14) gives the parable of the two bodies exactly as
Cicero reports it, and mentions Catiline's belief that there were
many in the senate πραγμάτων καινῶν ἐφιέμενοι.

The *comitia* had clearly been postponed with the definite object of allowing Cicero to make his statement, and, when that statement proved unconvincing, there was no further reason for postponement. The senate did not even think it necessary to provide Cicero with a bodyguard, as it had done for Cotta and Torquatus on a previous occasion. Cicero therefore had no alternative but to proceed at once with the elections, making what arrangements he could for his safety and the maintenance of order. The plot to murder him had been deranged by the change of date, but was likely to be repeated, and therefore Cicero on the actual day of election was attended by a strong band of armed friends and clients, and ostentatiously wore a breastplate under his toga. While Sallust and Dio Cassius do not think it worth while to mention the brief postponement at all, Plutarch evidently gathered from his authorities that the election followed at once after the meeting of the senate. In the same sentence in which Catiline's parable of the two bodies is referred to, he goes on : μᾶλλον ὁ Κικέρων ἔδεισε, καὶ τεθωρακισμένον αὐτὸν οἵ τε δυνατοὶ πάντες ἀπὸ τῆς οἰκίας καὶ τῶν νέων πολλοὶ κατήγαγον εἰς τὸ πεδίον . . . οἱ δ' ἠγανάκτουν καὶ συνεστρέφοντο περὶ αὐτόν· καὶ τέλος ἐν ταῖς ψήφοις τὸν μὲν Κατιλείναν αὖθις ἐξέβαλον. The same immediate sequence of events is made still clearer and more unimpeachable by Cicero himself (*pro Mur.* 26, 52), who in the sentence following the incident in the senate, goes on : *his tum rebus commotus et quod homines iam tum coniuratos cum gladiis in campum deduci a Catilina sciebam, descendi in campum cum firmissimo praesidio fortissimorum virorum et cum illa lata insignique lorica . . . Itaque cum te, Servi, remissiorem in petitione putarent, Catilinam et spe et cupiditate inflammatum viderent, omnes, qui illam a republica pestem depellere cupiebant, ad Murenam se statim contulerunt. Magna est autem comitiis consularibus repentina voluntatum inclinatio,* etc.

I have never understood on what grounds Mommsen, followed by other historians, believed the elections to have been postponed till October. What, on this supposition, was happening during the two intervening months ? The senate would only have consented to such a postponement if Cicero had convinced it of the existence of a real and dangerous conspiracy. Its refusal to take action proves that he did not do this, and if there had been such a conspiracy, it would have grown during the delay, and would have all the more called for government action, when after the postponement the *comitia* came on. Instead of this, we find exactly the same situation, Cicero still having only his band of personal friends to depend on, and the senate and the public still unconscious of an impending revolution. This is certain, if Cicero's evidence is of any value at all, for next year he declares : *vos enim tum* (at the time of the elections) *nihil laborabatis neque suspicabamini* (*pro Sull.* 51). As far as I can see, there is only one expression in the authorities which might be taken to imply that the elections were later than July. Plutarch says that the incident of Crassus bringing the letters to Cicero's house was not long after the elections, οὐ πολλῷ ὑστέρον, but this elastic phrase means little in Plutarch, and is far outweighed by the clear account of the elections which has preceded. I do not know by what arguments C. John has convinced Mr. Heitland that Mommsen is wrong, but I am sure that both the evidence and the situation necessitate this conclusion.

It is not clear that any actual attempt was made on the day of the *comitia* at either assassination or forcible interruption. It is true that Cicero charges Catiline with having wished to kill him and the rival candidates, and declares that he suppressed the attempt, but he adds : *nullo tumultu publice concitato* (*in Cat.* i, 11). Similarly, though he speaks of the *conatum Autroni et Catilinae, cum in campo comitiis consularibus, quae a me habita sunt, caedem facere voluerunt*, and declares that he saw Autronius in the *campus*, he implies that no one else noticed him, so that there can have been no disturbance (*pro Sull.* 51). There is, in fact, no objection to Dio's statement as true for the moment, that οἱ συνωμοκότες τῷ Κατιλείνᾳ φοβηθέντες αὐτὸν ἡσύχασαν (c. 29 *ad fin.*).

A careful consideration of the evidence therefore leads to the conclusion that the consular elections were held as usual some time in July, after only a few days' postponement. Though Cicero had failed to persuade the senate of a dangerous conspiracy, there must nevertheless have been very general alarm among the richer and more orderly classes both at Catiline's public utterances and at the riotous crowds of old Sullan soldiers who had been marshalled in to vote for him. If Catiline had really hoped or intended to further his cause by riot or assassination, he found his way blocked by the consul's precautions, which no doubt had, as they were meant to have, considerable effect upon the mass of voters. Whether, in consequence of recent developments, the expected support of the popular leaders was withdrawn, is a matter for conjecture; but at any rate, in spite of extreme and persistent efforts, and notwithstanding the fact that his competitors were insignificant and divided, the result was once more against him, and Silanus and Murena were elected.

It is curious that up to this point we have received very little dependable help from Sallust. But he makes two statements in c. 26 concerning Antonius which may be considered here. He says that Catiline hoped *si designatus foret, se ex voluntate Antonio usurum.* Let us put side by side with this (1) Cicero's description of Catiline as *inflatum . . . conlegae mei, quemadmodum dicebat ipse, promissis* (*pro Mur.* 49), and (2) Dio's assertion that Catiline wished to kill Cicero on the day of election ἵν' ὕπατος εὐθὺς χειροτονηθῇ. We might be tempted to infer that, if Catiline had been elected, and Cicero killed, the former and Antonius would have held the consulship together during the rest of the year.

But the evidence appears too slight to support such a conclusion. The scheme would have amounted to a *coup d'état*, and for this to have had any chance of success it must have had the support of the popular leaders. The hypothesis of such support seems to me to be contrary to all the indications and probabilities of the case. As far as Catiline was concerned, it is probable that, since Cicero's unrestrained denunciation of him in the summer of 64, he would have taken any opportunity to assassinate Cicero. It was just because, in spite of much unscrupulous ability, his unregulated passions were always bringing him down to the level of a mere assassin, that he proved in the end an unsuitable instrument for Caesar's purposes. But the evidence for this particular murder scheme is hardly worth considering. Cicero indeed asserted that there was such a plot, but the admissions involved in what he did and what he said deprive this assertion of all value. He omitted to mention it in the senate, which can only have been because he had no sufficient evidence. On the day when the murder was to have been carried out, all he can say is that he saw Autronius in the *campus*. He never pretends that there was any armed gathering, or any attempt actually made. Even the breastplate, which he put on, he admits was not to protect his life, but to create the impression that his life was in danger. *Descendi in campum . . . cum illa lata insignique lorica, non quae me tegeret, . . . verum ut omnes boni animadverterent*, etc. (*pro Mur.* 52).

But though the evidence against Catiline on this charge of attempted murder will not bear sifting, Cicero's information may have been well founded. In that case, Caesar and Crassus either knew of the plot or they did not. If they did, and if Catiline had shown himself up to this point the capable and adaptable instrument which they had originally hoped to find in him, it might be suggested, though I do not myself accept the suggestion, that they would not have vetoed the murder of Cicero, but would have taken advantage of it to establish the situation in July which they had originally hoped for in January. But Catiline's language in the *contio* and the senate, though it does not go far towards proving the existence of a *coniuratio*, shows a distinct disposition to

take the bit between his teeth, and to shake off the guiding
reins of the popular leaders. But if, on the other hand,
the latter were wholly unconcerned in the matter, or kept
in the dark, it would have been a mere murderous outrage
on the part of Catiline and his friends, which, whether
Antonius joined in it or not, could have led to no
consequences incapable of being dealt with.

Sallust's second statement raises the question as to the
position of Antonius. On this the evidence is somewhat
conflicting. It is sometimes assumed that, even before
entering on the consulship, Cicero had detached his colleague from Catiline by renouncing his claim to Macedonia.

For this I can find no evidence whatever. We have
already seen that both Dio Cassius and Plutarch represent
Antonius as interested in and supporting the agrarian
proposal of Rullus, though the latter apparently believes
(c. 12) that it was on this occasion that Cicero, as he
puts it, ἐκείνῳ ἐψηφίσατο τῶν ἐπαρχιῶν Μακεδονίαν. On the
other hand, Sallust in c. 26, speaking of the situation
just before the elections, says : *ad hoc conlegam suum
Antonium pactione provinciae perpulerat ne contra rempublicam sentiret*, a statement which, from its context, seems
to place the arrangement at this time. That it was not
earlier than this is implied by Cicero himself, who (*pro
Mur.* 49) speaks of Catiline in his canvass as relying on the
promises of Antonius, while in his list of consular speeches,
evidently given in their time order (*ad Att.* ii, 1, 3), sixth
in order, and immediately before the first against Catiline,
comes that *cum provinciam in contione deposui.*[1] But there
seems no particular reason why Cicero should have made
the *pactio* with Antonius in connexion with the elections,

[1] The inference from the order of the speeches is on the whole
confirmed by *in Pison.* 2, 5, where, after enumerating other acts of
his consulship, he says : *ego Antonium conlegam, cupidum provinciae, multa in republica molientem . . . mitigavi ; ego
provinciam Galliam . . . quam cum Antonio commutavi,
. . . in contione deposui.* The transfer of Macedonia and the
relinquishment of Gaul were two steps probably taken at the same
time, though Dio's narrative, referred to below, obscures this.

and on the whole I believe that Dio is confusedly following
good authority when he places the incident after Catiline's
departure from Rome in November. That Dio regards
Antonius as still dangerously implicated with Catiline after
the elections is shown by his reported presence at the
meeting of conspirators in which the programme of the
conspiracy is put forward (D. C. xxxvii, 30). But far
more important than the story of the meeting, which is
partly discredited by the silly tradition of the oath ad-
ministered over the heart of a murdered child, are the
statements made in c. 33. When it was announced that
Catiline had joined Manlius, οἱ Ρωμαῖοι τήν τε βίαν αὐτοῦ
κατεψηφίσαντο καὶ τὸν Ἀντώνιον ἐς τὸν πόλεμον . . . ἔστειλαν.
Cicero remained behind, εἰλήχει γὰρ τῆς Μακεδονίας ἄρξαι,
οὔτε δὲ ἐς ἐκείνην (τῷ γὰρ συνάρχοντι αὐτῆς διὰ τὴν περὶ τὰς δίκας
σπουδὴν ἐξέστη) οὔτε ἐς τὴν Γαλατίαν τὴν πλησίον, ἣν ἀντέλαβε,
διὰ τὰ παρόντα ἐξήλασεν ἀλλὰ κ. τ. λ. The passage is in
several respects confused. Dio distinguishes between a
general reason διὰ τὴν περὶ τὰς δίκας σπουδήν for resigning
Macedonia and a special reason διὰ τὰ παρόντα for giving
up Gaul, and evidently imagines that, if he had taken
Gaul, he would have had to leave Rome at once, instead
of at the end of the year. The special cause for settling
the question of the provinces was clearly the declaration
of Catiline and Manlius as public enemies, an act somewhat
obscurely described as τὴν βίαν αὐτοῦ κατεψηφίσαντο. This
virtually necessitated the sending out of one consul, and
Cicero was therefore forced at all costs to secure the
loyalty of Antonius, which he did by the bait of Macedonia
at the same time resigning Gaul to Metellus Celer for
another special reason, which we shall see later. In spite,
therefore, of Sallust's statement, it seems best to regard
Antonius as a possibly dangerous and hostile factor during
the critical period of the consular elections.

VI.

The Consilium Reipublicae Opprimendae and the Last Decree

WE have now reached what seemed the turning point in Catiline's career. If, without the outrage of Cicero's murder, he had been elected consul, it is probable, notwithstanding some irresponsible speeches and a tendency to take up an independent line, that in the next six months a *rapprochement* would have come about between him and the popular leaders, who might have convinced him that there was less to gain by running off the lines than by adhering to the programme of the previous year. But Catiline had been for the second time defeated. The new *ambitus* law was no doubt against him; Cicero had gained fresh influence since the previous year, and his ostentatious precautions would not be without their effect on the public mind; the monied classes may have been alarmed by indiscreet utterances; the optimatist candidates certainly made the most of Catiline's dangerous character, while, though Cicero rather keeps this point in the background, they were themselves supported by the soldiers of Lucullus, whose triumph was held about the time of the elections.[1] To these disadvantages, I am inclined to conjecture, should be added the withdrawal, perhaps at the last moment, of the support of Crassus and Caesar. The position of the popular leaders during the remainder of the year is, as already hinted, involved in much obscurity, but I suspect that new prospects were opened out to them about this time, which made them ready enough to acquiesce in the election of any two

---

[1] Speaking of Murena's supporters, Cicero says : *omitto clientes, vicinos, tribules, exercitum totum Luculli qui ad triumphum per eos dies venerant (pro Mur.* 33, 69). It was therefore not Catiline alone who was *inflatus spe militum.*

of the not very formidable senatorial candidates. I will only notice at the moment that Caesar had secured a place among the *praetores designati*, and that Metellus Nepos, fresh from Pompey's camp, had been elected one of next year's tribunes. It is the latter fact which in my opinion must furnish the clue to the attitude of the popular leaders towards what followed.

That his second defeat changed Catiline's plans and aims is expressed in different ways by Sallust and Dio Cassius. The former says (c. 26) : *constituit bellum facere et extrema omnia experiri, quoniam quae occulte temptaverat aspera foedaque evenerant.* The latter (xxxvii, 30) shows a far truer conception of the situation. καὶ ἐκεῖνος οὐκέτι λάθρα, οὐδὲ ἐπὶ τὸν Κικέρωνα τούς τε σὺν αὐτῷ μόνους, ἀλλὰ καὶ ἐπὶ πᾶν τὸ κοινὸν τὴν ἐπιβουλὴν συνίστη.[1] It seems to me that, excluding Sallust, all the evidence we have goes to confirm this statement of Dio. So far Catiline may have made repeated attempts on Cicero's life, but the motive had been personal hostility and desire to remove the chief obstacle in the way of the consulship. The consulship had been his main object, whether to be used in the service of others, with of course tangible rewards at the end of it, or, as was perhaps his latest idea, as the means of independent and revolutionary adventure. But in the course of his candidature he had undoubtedly formed connexions, primarily for electoral purposes, with discontented and impoverished country voters, while his masterful and pernicious personality had collected round him in Rome a dangerous and disorderly gang of what by courtesy we may term election agents. The inducements to support him, which a man of Catiline's antecedents would not hesitate to hold out, it is not difficult to conjecture.

---

[1] Cicero himself (*in Cat.* i, 12), after alluding to the attempted assassination at the elections, says : *nunc iam aperte rempublicam universam petis.* He adds with an obvious exaggeration, which makes the statement worthless : *templa deorum . . ., tecta urbis, vitam omnium civium, Italiam totam ad exitium ac vastitatem vocas.*

The course of events between the elections in July and October 21, the date on which the senate passed its last decree, it is somewhat difficult to determine. But in considering the evidence, it will be best to let Sallust make his statement first. *Igitur C. Manlium Faesulas atque in eam partem Etruriae, Septimium . . . in agrum Picenum, C. Iulium in Apuliam, . . . dimisit. Interea Romae multa simul moliri, consulibus insidias tendere, parare incendia, opportuna loca armatis hominibus obsidere, ipse cum telo esse, alios iubere hortari uti intenti paratique essent, . . . postremo, ubi multa agitanti nihil procedit, rursus intempesta nocte coniurationis principes convocat penes M. Porcium Laecam*, etc. (c. 27).

The passage is of little use to us, for Sallust not only puts the meeting at Laeca's house before October 21, whereas its real date was November 6, but sums up without discrimination the plans of three months, including some only arrived at on the occasion of that ante-dated meeting. We may, however, accept the statement that Manlius, Catiline's election agent, was sent back to Etruria with the soldiers and colonists who had come up to vote at the *comitia*. Both Plutarch (c. 15) and Dio Cassius (c. 30) imply this, and speak of intrigues and plots in Etruria and other parts of Italy.

It is probable too that Catiline now did what Sallust (c. 24) attributed to the previous year, sent arms and money to Faesulae and elsewhere. But all these preparations must still have been secret, for there were clearly only vague rumours of them as late as the middle of October.

As to what happened in Rome, Dio is no doubt following the accepted version when he says that Catiline gathered round him τοὺς κακίστους καὶ καινῶν ἀεί ποτε πραγμάτων ἐπιθυμοῦντας from Rome and Italy, making promises of χρεῶν ἀποκοπὰς καὶ γῆς ἀναδασμούς. It would seem that Dio, with some aberrations, is following good authorities, and, according to his account, the existence of a political and social *coniuratio* dates from this point. Catiline was enraged at his defeat, desperate in his fortunes; he had long had a dangerous *clientele* of profligate young men, and in the course of his two years' canvass for the consulship he had become aware of widespread distress and discontent among several sections of the population both in Italy and in Rome. He had perhaps already thrown out to these vague hopes of better things which his consulship would inaugurate, and he now attempted to bring these ill-assorted forces together in a furious attack on the established order. He had no doubt before this had relations more or less questionable with men like Autronius and Vargunteius; but it was now, and not, as Sallust represents, a year earlier, that he definitely grouped round himself, as leaders of a revolutionary movement, Lentulus Sura,[1] Autronius, Cethegus, Gabinius, Statilius, Vargunteius and the rest, with Manlius as their principal agent outside the capital.

According to what was evidently the received version, a meeting of these men was held in which Catiline explained his general plans, and perhaps, if we attach any value to Plutarch's phrase τῆς ὡρισμένης πρὸς τὴν ἐπίθεσιν ἡμέρας ἐγγύς, fixed a provisional day for the outbreak (Plut. *Cic.* 15). Sallust places this meeting some fourteen months too soon, but is wisely sceptical as to the story of human blood being drunk. Dio correctly dates it, but may be wrong in making Antonius take part in it, while he accepts and exaggerates the story of the hideous oath (c. 30).

That there were many disaffected elements within the body politic—to whom Catiline's propaganda of social and, above all, financial relief might appeal—is certain. Sallust indeed goes so far as to declare (c. 27), on the principle that the penniless always envy the rich, that *omnino cuncta plebes novarum rerum studio Catilinae incepta probabat.* The assertion is obviously far too sweeping, and is not justified by the superficial analysis which follows of the contemporary population of Rome.

But Cicero, though he spoke more from conjecture than knowledge, probably exposed correctly enough in his speech

[1] Both Plutarch and Dio introduce Lentulus as already praetor.

to the people on November 8 the kind of support which Catiline might look for. (1) There were the old soldiers and colonists of Sulla, who, having fallen into debt through extravagance, might hope for a fresh dictatorship and fresh proscriptions, while, roughly included in the same class, there were the rural populations at whose expense the Sullan soldiers had been provided for. In no part of Italy were conditions so acute as in Etruria, and it is not surprising that Faesulae and Arretium were the centres of the only rising which actually matured, though there were other parts, like Picenum and Apulia, which caused anxiety, and on which Catiline had his eye. (2) There was a miscellaneous class, both in Rome and in Italian towns, of small men who by bad luck or bad business had gone under, submerged by debt, and who would welcome any chance of relief. In spite of its numbers, this was not a formidable class, consisting of slackers rather than fighters, more ready to profit by a revolution than to run risks in bringing it about. (3) There was the criminal class, the *sicarii* and *parricidae*, ranging from the paid assassins employed in the Marian and Sullan massacres to broken and discredited men like Autronius and Vargunteius. Catiline knew well this kind of instrument, and, handled by himself, it was not to be despised. (4) There were Catiline's choice spirits, the dissolute fops and dandies whom he had corrupted and made his tools. Their gravest danger was that they constituted a *seminarium Catilinarum*. To these four classes, which undoubtedly contributed members to the conspiracy, Cicero adds (5) a class of men whom, though with large possessions, their extravagance or speculation had involved in debt. Rather than discharge this by selling their estates, they would allow themselves to hope for *novae tabulae*, though they were more likely to pray for a revolution than to take up arms. There is no evidence that men of this stamp joined Catiline, and Cicero's allusion to them was probably meant as a warning and manifesto to those whom be suspected of sitting on the fence. Catiline believed, and it was probably rumoured, that there were certain senators not indisposed to his schemes. If there were, they never committed themselves, and in including them in his list, Cicero must have been affecting more knowledge than he possessed (*in Cat.* ii, 18-23).[1]

We may assume, therefore, that a conspiracy was now under weigh, that Manlius was doing his best to raise a force in Etruria from the Sullan colonists and from the country population (Sall. c. 28); that emissaries were sent to Picenum, and that some steps were taken to rouse the slaves on the pastures of Apulia. The want of arms was probably the great difficulty, and Catiline made desperate efforts to raise money for their supply. In Rome things seem to have got little farther than the beating up of likely partisans, secret meetings and vague plans of assassination. The situation seems fairly summed up by Sallust: *multa agitanti nihil procedit.* It seems clear that Cicero was anxious and not at present well informed of what was going on. Sallust (c. 29) represents him as *ancipiti malo permotus.* He knew vaguely of plots in Rome, and felt the need of government support; he was aware of trouble in Etruria, but *exercitus Manlii quantus aut quo consilio foret, non satis compertum habebat.*

According to Sallust, Cicero in his uncertainty referred the danger at once to the senate; *rem ad senatum refert iam antea vulgi rumoribus exagitatum.* But he clearly at this point had no more than rumour to go upon, and he had experienced before the elections how impossible it was to induce the senate to take action on such information. We get better help from Plutarch and Dio Cassius. From these authorities it appears that Cicero's action in calling the senate was the result of information supplied to him by Crassus. Plutarch (*Cic.* 15) states that Crassus went

---

[1] Cicero mentions what he calls a sixth class, men *qui, quamquam premuntur aere alieno, dominationem tamen expectant, rerum potiri volunt,* hoping for positions amid disturbance which would be out of reach under normal conditions. I feel little doubt that the representative, probably the sole representative, of this class in Cicero's mind was Caesar.

to Cicero by night, accompanied by M. Marcellus and Metellus Scipio, and bringing a number of letters addressed to leading men, which had been mysteriously left at his house. The one addressed to himself he had opened, and found it to contain an unsigned warning of an impending massacre being prepared by Catiline. Dio Cassius (c. 31) tells the same story less in detail, while, what compels us to treat it seriously, Plutarch in his life of Crassus (c. 13) attributes the origin of the story to Cicero himself ἐν τῷ περὶ τῆς ὑπατείας λόγῳ.

On this, Cicero hurriedly called the senate, perhaps, as Plutarch describes, causing the other letters, whose contents proved to be identical, to be opened and read. At any rate, he laid the information before the senate. That body, no doubt taking into consideration rumours from Etruria, felt the information serious enough to vote, not indeed the ' last decree,' but a state of *tumultus*, and to order an investigation by the consul as to the reported plan of massacre. Dio, after alluding to the reports about Manlius in Etruria, says : μηνύεται τῷ Κικέρωνι πρότερα μὲν τὰ ἐν τῷ ἄστει γιγνόμενα διὰ γραμμάτων τινῶν, ἃ τὸν μὲν γράψαντα οὐκ ἐδήλου, τῷ δὲ δὴ Κράσσῳ καὶ ἄλλοις τισί τῶν δυνατῶν ἐδόθη, καὶ ἐπ' αὐτοῖς δόγμα ἐκυρώθη, ταραχήν τε εἶναι καὶ ζήτησιν τῶν αἰτίων αὐτῆς γενέσθαι. Somewhat later, more definite information reached Cicero of what was happening in Etruria, and it was on this that the senate passed its last decree : δεύτερα δὲ τὰ ἀπὸ τῆς Τυρσηνίδος, καὶ προσεψηφί-σαντο τοῖς ὑπάτοις τὴν φυλακὴν τῆς τε πόλεως καὶ τῶν ὅλων αὐτῆς πραγμάτων, καθάπερ εἰώθεσαν. I have quoted Dio's statement, because it seems clear and convincing, and removes more than one difficulty. Plutarch, like Sallust, knows of only one meeting of the senate, and represents the *senatus consultum ultimum* as passed when the letters were produced, at the same time making Q. Arrius, an ex-praetor, report that Manlius with an army was hovering round the Etruscan cities, waiting for news from Rome (c. 15 *ad fin.*).

But just as Sallust must have been wrong in placing the *s. c. ultimum* at a time when Cicero was without all definite information, so it is certain that the news brought by Arrius, clearly the news presented at Dio's second meeting of the senate (δεύτερα δὲ κ. τ. λ.), was not, as Plutarch makes it, the news of a definite rising on the part of Manlius. This is proved both by Cicero himself and by Sallust. In his first speech on November 7 Cicero says : *meministine me a.d. xii kal. Nov. dicere in senatu fore in armis certo die, qui dies futurus esset a.d. vi kal. Nov., C. Manlium ? . . . num me fefellit ? . . . dixi ego idem in senatu caedem te optimatium contulisse in a.d. v kal. Nov.* (*in Cat.* i, 7). This passage places it beyond doubt that on October 21, the date of the last decree, it was not yet known that Manlius had actually raised the standard of revolt. This is also proved by Sallust in c. 30, who relates that some days after the passing of the *s. c. ultimum* a letter was read in the senate by L. Saenius, announcing *C. Manlium arma cepisse cum magna multitudine a.d. vi kal. Nov.* On the other hand, it is perfectly clear that between the first meeting of the senate and that on October 21 Cicero had received new and important information. At the former meeting he had the merest rumours from Etruria, and only the vague warning contained in the anonymous letter to Crassus that a massacre in Rome was impending. On October 21 he was in possession of news from Arrius, not, as Plutarch says, no doubt confusing the message of Arrius with that of Saenius, that Manlius was under arms, but that he was timed to be so by October 27. Not only this, but he had now obtained far more definite clues to Catiline's designs in Rome, for he was able to predict the day fixed for the massacre and also for an attempt on the colony of Praeneste.

If, then, my interpretation of the evidence is accepted, Cicero's vague alarm and uncertainty were first relieved by the anonymous revelations brought to him by Crassus, which led to the first meeting of the senate, and its first decree, proclaiming a *tumultus* and ordering a special investigation. Then came fuller information both about Manlius and about the plot in Rome, and these being reported to a second meeting of the senate were the occasion of the ' last decree' being passed on October 21. There is reason to think that only two days elapsed between the two meetings. Asconius declares (*in Pison.* 6) that Cicero's first speech was delivered on the *octavus decimus dies* after the passing of the 'last decree.' This is certainly true, for the speech was on the day after the meeting at Laeca's house,[1] and that was on the night of November 6, *nocte ea quae consecuta est posterum diem Nonarum Novembrium* (*pro Sull.* 52). Thus October 21 to November 7 gives us, on the Roman method of counting, the *octavus decimus dies*. Why, then, does Cicero himself (*in Cat.* i, 4), after mentioning previous cases when the last decree had been followed by prompt action, go on to declare : *at nos vicesimum iam diem patimur hebescere aciem horum auctoritatis?* The explanation of Asconius, that it is an instance of Cicero's liking for round numbers, appears to me wholly inadmissible. It seems far more reasonable to suggest that, in his desire to emphasise the length of the interval, Cicero took as his *terminus a quo* not the second meeting at which the ' last decree' was passed, but the first, which was in a sense the starting point of the senatorial action.

It was in the two days' interval between these meetings, as I believe, that Cicero was put into communication with Fulvia and Curius. I am not sure that we may not push conjecture a step farther, and suggest that these two informers were introduced to the consul by Caesar. I base this suggestion on several considerations : (1) Cicero certainly had fresh and precise information before October 21 ;

---

[1] That the meeting at Laeca's house was on the night before the first speech is not only implied by all accounts, but is proved by Cicero's words : *recognosce tandem mecum noctem illam superiorem*, etc. (i, 8) coupled with the phrase *priore nocte* just after. It is true that Cicero says (i, 1) *quid proxima quid superiore nocte egeris ;* but here the meeting was held *proxima nocte*, the word *superiore* being always relative to a later *terminus*, here to *proxima*, in the other passage to the date of the speech. Cicero obviously only inserts *superiore* to convey the impression that he had been watching Catiline for days.

(2) he must have received it just after the strange intervention of Crassus; (3) it is safe to assume that Crassus did not act without the concurrence of Caesar; (4) Suetonius (*Iul.* 17) makes a statement best explained in the light of this suggestion. In this passage we are told that Curius was afterwards publicly rewarded *quod primus consilia coniuratorum detexerat.* After the conspiracy was put down, and while Caesar was under some suspicion owing to his opposition to the execution, Curius ventured in the senate to allude to Caesar's complicity with Catiline. Upon this, Caesar called on Cicero to testify *quaedam se de coniuratione ultro ad eum detulisse.* This, according to Suetonius, prevented Curius from receiving the decreed reward. Why Curius should have lost his reward for having mentioned Caesar, is not clear, unless indeed Cicero's evidence showed that Caesar's revelations to him had come through Curius, who had thus become first informer by Caesar's agency. That Caesar had his secret agents we may be sure, and it is not unlikely that he supplemented the vague warning of Crassus by passing on Curius and Fulvia to Cicero.

It was therefore not till the night of October 18 that Cicero obtained through Crassus information which he could use. On the 19th the senate passed a first and more or less tentative decree. During the next two days Cicero got more definite information, revealing a concerted plan for an almost simultaneous rising in Etruria and massacre in Rome, fixed for October 27 and 28 respectively. On the 21st the senate was sufficiently impressed by Cicero's confident predictions as to pass its last decree, *darent operam consules ne quid respublica detrimenti caperet.* The decree immensely strengthened Cicero's hands, and it was immediately ordered *uti Romae per totam urbem vigiliae haberentur, eisque minores magistratus praeessent.*[1]   (*Sall.*

[1] Sallust places these steps after the news from Etruria, but this could not have reached Rome before the 29th, and, as there was information of a massacre planned for the 28th, no time would have been lost, and Cicero explicitly states that he prevented the massacre by means of his guards (*in Cat.* i, 8).

c. 30). But while these extraordinary precautions seem effectually to have checked any immediate designs of sedition in Rome,[1] the situation was nevertheless unprecedented and dangerous. Never before had this extreme decree been passed merely in anticipation of a state of war, and in reliance upon unproved statements of a magistrate. The immediate result was a state of intense and feverish excitement ; *quibus rebus permota civitas atque immutata urbis facies; . . . festinare, trepidare, neque loco neque homini satis credere (Sall. c. 31)* ; and, when for some days nothing happened, there were many who suspected Cicero of having created a false alarm from motives of personal enmity to Catiline, ὥστε καὶ ἐπὶ συκοφαντίᾳ τὸν Κικέρωνα διαβληθῆναι (D. C. c. 31). But this interval of suspense was ended by the announcement of Saenius that Manlius had actually taken up arms on October 27,[2] while at the same time less definite reports came in of meditated slave disturbances in Apulia, and at Capua. Any immediate danger to the state had been averted by the senate's action on the 21st, which, if unprecedented at the time, was justified now in the face of an open enemy in the field. The real danger would have been a simultaneous movement in Rome and in Italy while the government was still unprepared for either. As it was, in the city the conspiracy was temporarily checked, while it was not difficult to take adequate measures against the danger from outside. Though no levy was yet ordered, two proconsuls, awaiting their triumph, Marcius Rex and Metellus Creticus, were directed to proceed in the direction of Faesulae and Apulia ; Metellus Celer was sent to Picenum, and another praetor to Capua. We get these arrangements from Sallust, and they are just the details which we may safely accept on his authority (*c.* 30 ; *conf. in Cat.* i, 8).

[1] Dio Cass. c. 31 : γενομένου δὲ τούτου καὶ φρουρᾶς πολλαχόθι καταστάσης τὰ μὲν ἐν τῷ ἄστει οὐκέτ᾽ ἐνεωτερίσθη.

[2] Whether Manlius really first took overt action exactly on this date, or whether Cicero arranged that the news should confirm his own prediction, is uncertain. He at any rate laid great stress on the verification of his date (i, 7).

At the same time Praeneste was put into a state of defence against an attack, planned, according to Cicero's information, for Nov. 1. As the numerous gladiators kept in Rome were a possible danger, they were distributed among the municipal towns, while, an indication that Cicero's amateur detective agency was inadequate, rewards were offered both to slaves and free men for further information.

VII.

The Conspiracy till the Ejection of Catiline

IT would seem that this favourable position of the
government at the end of October was largely due
to the action taken by Crassus, not without the
knowledge and perhaps the co-operation of Caesar. The
motive and exact nature of that action can only be con-
jectured, and, in framing a conjecture, I shall revert to
the situation earlier in the year, when the three courses
open to the popular leaders seemed to be (1) a second
attempt to secure executive agents among next year's
magistrates, (2) some kind of *coup d'état*, and (3) the estab-
lishment of a *modus vivendi* with Pompey. The first plan
had failed, because even before the elections Catiline had
either broken away from their control, or by his indis-
cretions had aroused so much influential opposition as to
ensure his defeat. The second course would be a last
resource, and the conditions were not at the moment
altogether favourable. The government with Cicero at its
head had been strong enough even at the beginning of the
year to defeat their schemes and foil their tactics. After
the elections Cicero was stronger than ever, while many of
the forces on which they would have to rely for a successful
coup were being won over by Catiline's unauthorised and
impossible propaganda. That Caesar, with his political
career to shape, and Crassus, with his vast financial
interests, were unaware of what was going on below the
surface, or that they would stand aside and allow the
established order to stand or fall with Cicero's unassisted
ability to maintain it, is of all suppositions the least
credible. Their reserve and almost ostentatious inactivity
can hardly have been other than the result of confidence
and conscious strength. Caesar had secured his election
to the praetorship for the next year, but that is not by

itself sufficient to account for this security. It must be
remembered that Metellus Nepos had come straight from
Pompey's head-quarters to stand for the tribuneship, and
that he had been elected. That Pompey could have hoped
by means of a single tribune to secure all that his interests
demanded, in the face of senatorial opposition and the
attitude of the popular leaders, it is impossible to believe.
It is far more probable, and the actions of Metellus at the
end of the year and the beginning of 62 confirm the suggestion, that Metellus was to be the intermediary of a more
or less definite understanding between Pompey on the one
hand and Crassus and Caesar on the other, which might
foreshadow an ultimate coalition. It was perhaps because
the *optimates* suspected something of the kind that they
induced Cato to stand for the tribuneship. Cicero clearly
foresaw dangers in the following year, and certainly not
merely from advocacy on the part of Metellus of Pompey's
interests, *Te, te appello, Cato, nonne prospicis tempestatem
anni tui? Iam enim in hesterna contione intonuit vox
perniciosa designati tribuni, conlegae tui, contra quem
multum tua mens, multum omnes boni providerunt, qui te
ad tribunatus petitionem vocaverunt* (*pro Mur.* 38, 81). It
is after all the menace from Pompey which best explains
the conduct of Crassus and Caesar during the past three
years, and on the hypothesis that a *modus vivendi* was now
in the way of being established with him, their behaviour
during the rest of the year becomes fully intelligible.

Catiline had broken away, and, whatever Cicero knew,
it may be safely assumed that his former employers would
make it their business to acquaint themselves with his
designs. Those designs were obviously not dangerous, if
adequately met. The result decisively proved this; it
was recognised by Cicero's own action in allowing Catiline
to leave Rome; and indeed the only danger would have
been, if the government's action in dealing with the external
menace had been crippled by a successful revolution in
Rome. To prevent the possibility of this danger, and
perhaps to supply the deficiencies of Cicero's intelligence

department, Crassus gave him timely warning. Dio says that he did this in order to escape suspicion on the score of his friendship with Catiline. This motive, however, must explain, not the warning itself, but the somewhat awkward form in which it was conveyed. If Crassus had merely caused an anonymous letter to be addressed to himself, it might have suggested some connexion with Catiline, but as others received similar letters, the risk of being compromised was avoided. Having thus put the government upon its guard, and seeing the consul in a position to take adequate measures by means of the senate's action, Caesar and Crassus could afford to await developments with equanimity. It was perhaps regrettable that the last decree had had to be acquiesced in, and it was mortifying to see certain extreme sections of the popular party incited to run amok with Catiline, while the affair might even bring some temporary discredit upon the whole party. But there was clear weather ahead beyond this cyclonic disturbance, and meanwhile there was every chance that the government might make some false step, and by straining or exceeding the legitimate application of the extreme decree once more give an opportunity for raising a popular cry.

Meanwhile the measures taken by Cicero had disconcerted Catiline's plans in Rome, and an accusation was set on foot against him under the *lex Plautia de vi*.[1] There was, however, as yet no evidence against him either of complicity with Manlius or of the murderous designs attributed to him by Cicero, and he ostentatiously prepared to meet the charge, offering to live in custody, first with M. Lepidus, then with Cicero himself, then with Metellus Celer, and, when all these refused to harbour him, living under surveillance with a certain M. Metellus.[2] Thus for some days things hung fire. Cicero had now plenty of information through Fulvia, but no proof, while Catiline

---

[1] Sall. c, 31 ; conf. Dio Cass. c. 31 : βίας ἐπ᾽ οὐτοῖς γραφὴν τῷ Κατιλείνᾳ παρεσκεύασαν.

[2] *In Cat.* i, 19 ; Dio (c. 32) confuses the two Metelli.

still received no news from Etruria to justify the risk of action in Rome. The cause of the delay lay no doubt with Manlius, whose numbers increased but slowly, though perhaps more quickly than the supply of arms and equipment. If he had been strong enough to strike, he would hardly have wasted time in futile appeals by letters to Marcius Rex complaining of the misery of debtors and the cruelty of usurers.[1]

Catiline had probably made up his mind by the first few days of November that, if any progress was to be made, he must himself take charge of the operations in Etruria. He determined, therefore, *exercitum augere ac, prius quam legiones scriberentur, multa antecapere quae bello usui forent* (c. 32). Cicero declares that he knew of this intention, and of the actual day fixed with Manlius, as well as of a silver eagle sent forward for the troops (*in Cat.* i, 24). Catiline on his part, still living with Metellus, was giving it out that, owing to the persecutions to which he was subject, he should retire into exile at Massilia (*in Cat.* ii, 14; Sall. c. 34).

On the night of November 6 Catiline called together the leaders of the conspiracy to the house of M. Porcius Laeca in the street of the Scythemakers. He there laid the situation before them, pointing out the dangers of further delay, and no doubt once more expatiating upon the rewards of success. For himself, he should go to Etruria, and prepare for an immediate march on Rome. Of the rest, some were to accompany their leader, others were assigned to different parts of Italy. Meanwhile the conspiracy in Rome was to proceed; the city was to be marked off into districts for systematic incendiarism, and, when the time came, there was to be a massacre of leading men. *Distribuisti partes Italiae, statuisti quo quemque proficisci placeret; deligisti quos Romae relinqueres, quos tecum educeres; descripsisti urbis partes ad incendia; confirmasti te ipsum iam exiturum; dixisti paulum tibi etiam nunc esse*

[1] Sall. cc. 33-4. It is uncertain whether the correspondence took place, or is the invention of Sallust.

morae, quod ego viverem ; reperti sunt duo equites Romani qui te ista cura liberarent, et sese illa ipsa nocte paulo ante lucem me in meo lectulo interfecturos sese pollicerentur (*in Cat.* i, 8).[1]   The one thing, therefore, which Catiline required to be done at once was the murder of Cicero, and this Cornelius and Vargunteius promised to accomplish on the same night.

We may accept from Cicero this programme of the conspiracy as formulated by Catiline himself on the night of November 6.   It is generally confirmed by Dio and Plutarch, though not in immediate connexion with the meeting.   According to the former (c. 34) it was καταπρῆσαί τέ τινας καὶ σφαγὰς ἐργάσασθαι.   The latter (c. 18) describes it as τὴν βουλὴν ἅπασαν ἀναιρεῖν τῶν τ' ἄλλων πολιτῶν ὅσους δύναιτο, τὴν πόλιν δ' αὐτὴν καταπιμπράναι. Sallust, as we have seen, had put the meeting before the elections, but he says (c. 32) that Catiline, before leaving Rome, *mandat quibus rebus possint opes factionis confirment, insidias consuli maturent, caedem incendia aliaque belli facinora parent.*   It is at this point, as it seems to me, that the idea of burning the city first becomes a part of the programme,[2] and it seems clear, both from general probability and perhaps from Dio's phrase, καταπρῆσαί τινας, that the plan, as arranged by Catiline, was not the immediate and general conflagration of the city, but the massacre of many leading men in their own houses, and, with the view of creating a universal panic, the burning of the houses themselves.   When Catiline had left, there were no doubt hot-headed members of the plot, like Cethegus, who were for carrying out these designs at once ; but for Catiline himself and probably for Lentulus,

---

[1] The passage in *pro Sull.* 19, 53 agrees with this.   Dio (c. 32) mentions the meeting, and the plan to kill Cicero, but otherwise merely represents Catiline as upbraiding them for the delay, which was clearly no more their fault than his own.

[2] Sallust of course, in accordance with his general scheme, puts this design much earlier.   He even makes Catiline leave Rome *quod ab incendio intelligebat urbem vigiliis munitam.*

these plans of murder and incendiarism were to be carefully timed so as to coincide with the advance of an armed force from the North.

The whole of these plans were communicated to Cicero on the very night of the meeting by Fulvia. How far her account·of the resolutions arrived at was accurate, it is impossible to say. In any case, it was not a formidable programme, except on the assumption that all the parts of it were accurately timed, and that the government did nothing more to forestall them. Cicero no doubt convinced himself, or at least tried to convince others, that the city was parcelled out, not that certain houses, marked out in different quarters, should be simultaneously set on fire, but that the whole regions were to be destroyed by fire; and that the massacre was to affect, not certain important persons, but all the senate, and at last all the citizens, including women and children.· No one who has studied Cicero's methods will be surprised at the hysterical passage in *pro Sull.* 19: *cum huius urbis, cum illorum delubrorum et templorum, cum puerorum infantium, cum matronarum et virginum venerant in mentem, cum illae infestae et funestae faces universumque totius urbis incendium, . . . cum caedes, cum civium cruor, cum cinis patriae versari ante oculos . . . coeperat,* etc.

But whether or not the plans of Catiline were misreported by Fulvia or exaggerated by Cicero, the warning as to his own safety was at once verified, for the two knights appeared at the consul's house, but found it closed and guarded against them. Later in the morning Cicero summoned the senate to meet in the temple of Iupiter Stator on the Palatine, a place easily secured by guards. Catiline, though aware that his plans had leaked out, determined to bluff the matter out, and came with the rest, sitting amid empty benches and shunned by all.

Cicero rose and delivered the first of the four extant speeches. I am not concerned with it as a piece of oratory or an effective exposure of Catiline's immediate designs. To Dio Cassius and Plutarch (xxxvii, 33; *Cic.* c. 16) its one point seemed that it ordered Catiline from Rome. That his departure was in fact the one thing which Cicero desired there can be no doubt ; he even allowed himself to say : *exire ex urbe iubet consul hostem*. But he was evidently in a dilemma. His outspoken exposure of Catiline's designs, the intended co-operation with Manlius, an open enemy, and the plans for murder and incendiarism in the city, might seem to have proved too much or too little. If Catiline should really withdraw to Massilia, as he had declared it his intention to do, what evidence was there beyond Fulvia's assertion to prove that he was not an innocent man, driven into exile by overbearing denunciations of the consul ? If on the other hand he should join Manlius in accordance with Cicero's prediction, he would be a declared and open enemy, and how could the consul, who had foreseen this, excuse himself for letting such an enemy escape ? Cicero emphatically declares that, on the precedent of consular action taken against C. Gracchus and Saturninus, he could have ordered Catiline to be led to death (*in Cat.* i, 21 foll.). Nevertheless he not only did not adopt this course, but allowed Catiline the most complete freedom either to seek a place of safety or to join an open enemy of the state. He excuses this inactive attitude on the ground that many people still disbelieved his statements, and would regard strong measures against Catiline as cruel and tyrannical. On the other hand, if only Catiline and his associates could be induced or driven to join Manlius, no one, even the most sceptical, could doubt their guilt ; the very seed or root of the evil could be destroyed without danger, and every one would confess *iure factum esse*. Two things are clear from the speech : (1) that Cicero had still, in spite of his confident assertions, no evidence conclusive enough to rely upon by which to connect Catiline and his friends in Rome with what was as yet the only overt act of hostility to the state ; and that therefore, notwithstanding his denial, he feared the odium of either arrest or execution.

It was obviously still a case of suspicion only, and, when

Cicero appeals to the precedent of Opimius, and declares that Gracchus was killed *ob quasdam seditionis suspiciones*, he was wilfully misstating the case, for Gracchus and his followers were open rioters under arms.[1]   (2) It is abundantly clear from the tone of the whole speech,[2] and even more than the second speech, delivered on the following day to the people, that at this point Cicero had little fear of the conspirators in Rome without Catiline to direct them, and none at all of Manlius and his army, even if Catiline should put himself at its head.

Catiline, on attempting some reply to this denunciation, was howled down with cries of ' brigand ' and ' parricide,' and hastily left the senate. The same night he left Rome for the North by the Via Aurelia, accompanied by only a few of his friends. How relieved Cicero was by Catiline's departure is shown by the exuberant tone of his speech to the people on November 8. It was a splendid victory, and the contemptible little army of Manlius and Catiline, collected *ex senibus desperatis, ex agresti luxuria, ex rusticis decoctoribus*, will be of no avail *prae Gallicanis legionibus, et hoc dilectu quem in agro Piceno et Gallico Q. Metellus habuit, et his copiis quae a nobis cotidie comparantur* (*in Cat.* ii, 4).

It is indeed not the army of Catiline that is to be feared, but those *qui exercitum deserunt*, the conspirators left behind in Rome. *Intus, intus, inquam, est equus Troianus, a quo nunquam me consule dormientes opprimemini* (*pro Mur.* 38). For the moment, those left behind have the fullest opportunity of following their leader, but if they stay, and ' if I detect *non solum factum sed inceptum ullum conatumve contra patriam*, they shall discover why the

---

[1] *in Cat.* i, 4. That Cicero did not dare to take the decisive step, he admits in i, 12, though he scouts the imputation of timidity in i, 19.

[2] Plutarch knew of Cicero's speech, as the following passages show. δεῖν γὰρ αὐτοῦ μὲν λόγοις, ἐκείνου δ᾽ ὅπλοις πολιτευομένου μέσον εἶναι τὸ τεῖχος (*Cic.* 16). *dummodo inter me atque te murus intersit* (*in Cat.* i, 10).

carcer exists ' (ii, 27). As a matter of fact, it was precisely because Cicero ultimately carried out this threat, and applied martial law to men whose treason consisted in intention and not in overt act, that protests were made and accusations threatened by Metellus Nepos and Clodius.

Before Catiline left Rome, he addressed, according to Sallust's account, letters to several leading men, to the effect that, unable to resist the unfounded charges of his enemies, and to avoid being a cause of civil strife, he was going into exile at Massilia. To Lutatius Catulus, however, in a communication, which Sallust professes to report verbatim, he openly announced : *publicam miserorum causam pro mea consuetudine suscepi.*

It is not clear, however, what motive at this last moment Catiline could have had for sending the former letters, the falsity of which a few hours would expose ; and, as the plea of going to Massilia is alluded to in Cicero's first speech, it is probable that Sallust is mistaken, and that these letters were sent round as a blind before the meeting at Laeca's house.

VIII.

The Exposure and Arrest

AT any rate, Catiline, on leaving Rome, proceeded at once to the Sullan colony of Arretium, and, after distributing arms in the neighbourhood, and assuming the *fasces* and *insignia* of a consul, joined Manlius in his camp near Faesulae (Sall. c. 36). It is probable that so far Manlius had no more than 2,000 men, of whom only one-fourth were armed (App. ii, 7; Sall. c. 56); but Catiline's presence was sure to increase the number, and therefore, when the news reached Rome, Catiline and Manlius were declared public enemies,[1] a day was fixed within which any of the other rebels might earn pardon by deserting, and a more regular levy was set on foot (Sall. c. 36).[2] The proper person to command the new force was obviously the other consul, and it was probably now and not before that Cicero definitely secured the loyalty of Antonius by an exchange of province, Macedonia, which had fallen to Cicero, being relinquished to Antonius instead of Cisalpine Gaul.[3] Marcius Rex therefore must have been superseded at this point by Antonius, who marched North with a strong army in the course of November. It was apparently at the same time that Cicero, at no real cost to himself, attempted to disarm the threatened opposition of Metellus Nepos by conciliating his

[1] I interpret Dio's words τήν τε βίαν αὐτοῦ κατεψηφίσαντο as referring to Catiline's proclamation as a public enemy, and not to his condemnation under the *lex Plautia de vi.*

[2] Two things should be remembered: (1) that only Catiline and Manlius were affected by this declaration; (2) that it was not a necessary or even usual sequel to the *s. c. ultimum,* which was itself a declaration that all citizens in arms or open resistance to the state may be dealt with as public enemies.

[3] The passages bearing upon Antonius and Macedonia have already been considered above, p. 47 and foll.

brother Metellus Celer. The latter, as we have seen, was already in command of an army in Picenum, and Cicero, having no desire for a province, not only formally resigned his claim to Cisalpine Gaul, but with the help of Antonius so manipulated the *sortitio* among the praetors that it fell to Metellus. No other inference can be drawn from Cicero's own statement to Metellus. *Illud dico, me, ut primum provinciam in contione deposuerim, statim, quem ad modum eam tibi traderem, cogitare coepisse. Nihil dico de sortitione vestra; tantum te suspicari volo, nihil in ea re per conlegam meum me insciente esse factum (ad fam.* v, 2, 3). Dio Cassius (c. 33) is aware of the transaction, though he supposes that Metellus was to be sent to Gaul at once instead of at the end of the year. ἐς δὲ τὴν Γαλατίαν τὸν Μέτελλον, ὅπως μὴ καὶ ὁ Κατιλείνας αὐτὴν σφετερίσηται, ἔπεμψεν.[1]

It is not possible to trace with clearness the course of events either in North Italy or in Rome between November 8 and the beginning of December.[2] It is clear that Cicero, though relieved at Catiline's departure, was disappointed to find that his most dangerous associates had remained behind. *Aut reliquam coniuratorum manum simul exituram, aut eos, qui restitissent, infirmos sine illo ac debiles fore putavi (in Cat.* iii, 4).

It is equally clear that he had not convinced either the people or the senate that massacre and incendiarism were seriously being prepared in Rome. Speaking of the effect of his second speech, he says : *cum auribus vestris propter incredibilem magnitudinem sceleris minorem fidem faceret*

---

[1] We are told by Sallust (c. 42) that C. Murena, brother of the consul designate, was acting as *legatus* in Gallia Citerior. But it is clear from *pro Mur.* 41, 89 that he was legate to his brother, who was governor of Transalpine Gaul. Unless Sallust has made a mistake, Murena was perhaps governor of both Gauls for the time. At any rate, if Cisalpine Gaul was not under Murena, there is nothing to show who held it before Metellus.

[2] Cicero in the third speech and Sallust are the authorities for what follows, usefully supplementing one another. Dio's account of the affair of the Allobroges is lost.

oratio mea. He therefore spent day and night in trying to discover more precise information. The difficulty was probably greater, because, after the revelations made on the night of November 6, the conspirators would be more careful, and Fulvia was no longer available. As a matter of fact, the next clue came by pure good fortune. Lentulus and his friends must have been almost as embarrassed as Cicero, for, though the impetuous Cethegus urged immediate action, it cannot be doubted that Catiline's instructions were for the rising in the city and his own advance upon it to be simultaneous. That advance, however, was soon found to be as hopeless as Cicero had foreseen it would be. Ultimately something like 20,000 men (*App.* ii, 7) or at least enough to make up two full legions (Sall. c. 56) were collected in Etruria, but out of these only one-fourth part was armed, and against them were the armies of Antonius and Metellus, as well as the forces of Cisalpine Gaul, if it should be necessary to employ them. Week after week therefore passed, and, though Lentulus may have gained a few more accomplices, nothing happened, and the city, though paraded by Cicero's guards, was tranquil enough to watch with interest the trial of Murena, one of the consuls designate.

It speaks little for Cato, as a practical politician, that he should have supported Servius Sulpicius, the defeated competitor of Murena, in prosecuting the latter for breaches of the new *lex Tullia.* Sulpicius was a great lawyer, but on this occasion showed himself a hopeless pedant, and perhaps Cicero's elephantine witticisms on the eccentricities of doctrinaire jurisconsults met the case, as far as he was concerned. Cato's action in the matter is more difficult to explain. Not only had he been elected tribune to meet an expected combination against the senatorial party, but a week or two later he argued that nothing could save the state but a summary violation of the *lex Porcia* ; and yet by his present action he ran the risk of dividing his own party, and perhaps of leaving the republic with only one consul to face the anticipated dangers of the coming year. Cicero pointed out this danger with force and justice, and these redeeming passages in the dullest of dull speeches secured Murena's acquittal.

Towards the close of November the possibility was suggested to Lentulus of expediting Catiline's movements by means of aid from outside. There were in Rome some envoys from the Allobroges, who had come to seek relief at the hands of the senate from heavy public debt and the avarice of Roman magistrates. These were approached by Umbrenus, a freedman, who had held some financial post in Further Gaul, and who hinted at some more efficacious relief than was likely to be obtained from the senate. Then Gabinius took the matter up ; a meeting was arranged with the leading conspirators, and according to Sallust, the facts of the conspiracy were disclosed to them, as well as the names of those concerned in it. The Allobroges were promised relief from debt, as well as apparently political independence, while this *male pacata civitas* was to initiate ' a Transalpine war and Gallic tumult,' or more specifically, to send a force of Gallic cavalry into Italy in order to make Catiline's army more mobile.[1]

The envoys were made to believe that the conspiracy was supported by many who had no share in it, and the meeting ended with a promise on their part to recommend the scheme to their government.[2] But *vicit fortuna reipublicae* ; for they consulted Fabius Sanga, the patron of their state, who at once disclosed the matter to Cicero. He of course with his armed force had the envoys at his mercy, and compelled them to act as his agents and informers. They were in effect to continue their negotiations with the conspirators· with a view of obtaining conclusive proofs. Accordingly, in order to satisfy their

[1] Cicero and Sallust both state the wider object, but it appears that the Allobroges in their evidence only mentioned the stipulated despatch of cavalry (*in Cat.* iii, 4 and 9 ; Sall. c. 40).

[2] According to Sallust, *nominat multos cuiusque generis innoxios, quo legatis animus amplior esset.*

government, they demanded a solemn oath, written,
signed and sealed by each of the leading conspirators.
With incredible recklessness these fell into the trap, and
Lentulus, Cethegus, Gabinius and Statilius hopelessly
compromised themselves by giving the required pledge.
Autronius had already left Rome for Etruria (*pro Sull.*
17 and 53), while Cassius Longinus had started to give his
pledge in person to the Gallic *civitas*.

The whole scheme gives us the measure of the men who
were going to wage *bellum intestinum ac domesticum post
hominum memoriam crudelissimum et maximum.* For
even if ordinary precautions had been taken against
discovery, and if the envoys had conveyed their messages
to Catiline and reached home, the chances, first of a serious
rising in Further Gaul, and then of a successful cavalry
raid through the Cisalpine in the face of legions in both
provinces, were not worth considering. The fact was that
the only capable leader was cut off in Etruria. His agents
in Rome held midnight meetings and sent out arms, but,
as Sallust says, this caused *plus timoris quam periculi*,
while sporadic and ill considered attempts at disturbance
in Picenum and Apulia, perhaps even in the two Gauls,
only led to the arrest of Catiline's emissaries (Sall. c. 42).
The one redeeming point in the leadership of Lentulus is,
what is usually made a charge against him, his resistance
to the mad impatience of Cethegus. His plan still was
in the main what Catiline had arranged, that the attempt
in Rome was to be simultaneous with the approach of the
army from Etruria. Under no other circumstances could
there have been any hope of success.

As November drew to an end, it became clear that no
date could be safely fixed upon earlier than the second half
of December, and, according to the evidence of the Allobroges, the time of the Saturnalia was talked about (*in
Cat.* iii, 9). But Sallust is no doubt correct in making the
date provisional on the advance of the army. It was
arranged, he says (c. 43), *uti cum Catilina in agrum Faesulanum cum exercitu venisset, L. Bestia, tr. pl., contione*

habita, quereretur de actionibus Ciceronis, bellique . . .
invidiam . . . consuli imponeret; eo signo proxima
nocte cetera multitudo coniurationis suum quisque negotium
exsequeretur. This points to a date at any rate later than
December 10, when Bestia would become tribune, and,
on the supposition that cavalry from the Allobroges were
to co-operate with Catiline in his advance, no earlier date
could have been contemplated.[1] But Sallust is evidently
guilty of some confusion in the words *in agrum Faesulanum,*
for that had been the head-quarters of the insurgent army
ever since October. Besides, Faesulae was so far from
Rome that the army starting from there could not, even
without opposition, have reached the capital in time to
co-operate on the night after Bestia's meeting with the
rising in Rome. It seems obvious, therefore, that the
real objective of the army must have been some place
not many miles outside Rome.[2] We do less than justice
both to Catiline and Lentulus unless we bear in mind that
their plan depended throughout on concerted and simultaneous action on the part of the army and the conspirators
in the city. The original scheme had been for Manlius
to reach Rome by the end of October, before an army was
ready to meet him, and while Catiline was himself directing
affairs in the city. This plan was foiled by the revelations
made to Cicero in the middle of the month, in consequence
of which Catiline was compelled himself to join Manlius.
But it was then too late, for the advance on Rome was
blocked by armies continually becoming stronger. That,
of course, was the legitimate effect of the *s. c. ultimum.*
These armies still blocked Catiline's way; but on the
impossible supposition of Catiline's evading or breaking

[1] Appian (ii, 3) follows Sallust in the matter of the meeting to
be called by Bestia. But he has hopelessly confused the date.
He places it immediately after Catiline's departure, and so before
Bestia was tribune. He also confuses the attempt on Cicero's
life on November 7 with the part which Cethegus was to have
played in the rising on the Saturnalia.

[2] Mr. Warde Fowler suggests that *ad agrum Falerianum* would
suit my proposed correction of Sallust.

through them, there might still be a catastrophe. For, while Cethegus was set apart to murder Cicero and others, Gabinius and Statilius were to cause fires to break out in twelve different parts of the city with the view of causing a general panic, amid which the conspirators within and the army from outside were to join forces. We have already seen that Sallust is inclined to antedate the plan of burning the city, but in c. 43 he gives a sane and clear account of the final arrangements of Lentulus, which discounts much of Cicero's exaggerated talk about a general massacre and an *incendium totius urbis*. He says: *Sed ea divisa hoc modo dicebantur : Statilius et Gabinius uti cum magna manu duodecim simul opportuna loca urbis incenderent, quo tumultu facilior aditus ad consulem ceterosque quibus insidiae parabantur fieret; Cethegus Ciceronis ianuam obsideret eumque adgrederetur, alius autem alium, . . . simul caede et incendio perculsis omnibus, ad Catilinam erumperent.* The value of this passage as evidence is not weakened by the fact that it is not in entire agreement with Cicero's statement both in *pro Sull.* 53 and *in Cat.* iv, 13, where the work of incendiarism is specially assigned to Cassius Longinus. I have already suggested that Fulvia's information may have failed Cicero after November 7, and this discrepancy makes this the more probable. From the first speech it is clear that Cicero had been informed by Fulvia of the parts to be played by the several conspirators, that of Cassius being no doubt the direction of the incendiarism. But this detail had to be changed when Cassius left for Gaul, and therefore Cicero's statement, depending on Fulvia's original story, was not quite up to date. We may safely accept from Sallust (1) that in spite of Cethegus there was to be no rising until the army was within striking distance ; and (2) that the massacre and incendiarism were merely to cause a general panic.

These, then, were the plans of Lentulus and the other conspirators when, on the night of December 2, the envoys of the Allobroges left Rome. They had in their possession pledges to their government signed by Lentulus, Cethegus,

Gabinius and Statilius, and they were accompanied by Volturcius, a native of Croton, who was charged with a letter and a verbal message from Lentulus to Catiline. The envoys were to interview the latter and receive from him his confirmation of the compact. All this was known to Cicero, who now saw his way to obtain documentary proof of the conspirators' designs. He accordingly instructed two praetors, L. Flaccus and C. Pomptinus, to waylay the whole party at the Mulvian bridge. (Sall. c. 45; *in Cat.* iii, 6.) This was successfully accomplished, and the Allobroges, who had supplied the necessary information, and Volturcius with all the letters were secured. We can well believe Sallust's account of Cicero's mingled feelings. The time had come to take some responsible step. At break of day he summoned the senate to the temple of Concord, and meanwhile ordered Lentulus, Cethegus, Gabinius, Statilius and Caeparius to be arrested and brought to his own house. The first four duly appeared, though Caeparius, who was to have gone to Apulia, had for the moment escaped. In order to secure publicity for the exact evidence to be given, Cicero commissioned four senators of repute to take a verbatim report of it, to be entered in the public records, and subsequently published throughout Rome and Italy (*pro Sull.* 40 and 41).

These preparations being made, Cicero led the four arrested men to the temple of Concord. Volturcius was first introduced, and for us his evidence is the most important, because, unlike the Allobroges, he had had no previous communication with Cicero, and could not have been instructed, as they may have been, what to say, or whom to incriminate or pass over. On a free pardon being promised him, he apparently told all he knew, but, as he had only been admitted to the conspiracy a few days before by Gabinius, he knew little more than the envoys. Still, he was in possession of a letter from Lentulus to Catiline, and also the bearer of a verbal message. The letter is given in almost identical terms by Sallust (c. 44)

and Cicero (*in Cat.* iii, 12), the former no doubt taking it
from the published report, the latter quoting to the people
from memory. It ran : *Quis sim ex eo quem ad te misi
cognosces. Fac cogites, in quanta calamitate sis, et mem-
ineris te virum esse ; consideres quid tuae rationes postulent ;
auxilium petas ab omnibus, etiam ab infimis.* This merely
proved an understanding of some kind between Lentulus
and Catiline, a public enemy. The verbal message,
elicited from the evidence of Volturcius, is also given by
our two authorities, but the difference in their versions
is instructive. According to Sallust, who presumably used
Cicero's own official report, it was : *cum ab senatu hostis
iudicatus sit, quo consilio servitia repudiet ? in urbe parata
esse quae iusserit ; ne cunctetur ipse propius accedere.*
According to Cicero it was : *ut servorum praesidio uteretur ;
ut ad urbem quam primum cum exercitu accederet ; id
autem eo consilio, ut cum urbem ex omnibus partibus,
quemadmodum descriptum distributumque erat, incendissent
caedemque infinitam fecissent, praesto esset ille qui et fugientes
exciperet, et se cum his urbanis ducibus coniungeret.* Of
these two versions, no one can hesitate to prefer that of
Sallust. To suppose that Lentulus would have informed
Catiline through Volturcius of the plans for organised
murder and incendiarism, as to which Catiline had himself
given detailed instructions before leaving Rome, is absurd,
though it would be perfectly natural to say that the plans
arranged for were ready. Cicero is obviously not merely
quoting the message, but explaining to the people the
nature of the plans alluded to. He had known these a
month ago from Fulvia, but in his previous speeches he had
very imperfectly convinced either senate or people of their
truth. He now serves the same story up again, just as
he had heard it from Fulvia, with the *descriptio* and
distributio of the city (conf. i, 4, 9) and with the detail
about Cassius Longinus, which was no longer true, but he
conveys at the same time the impression that the story
is now confirmed by Volturcius, the emissary of Lentulus
to Catiline. It is not stated by either Sallust or Cicero

that Volturcius divulged more than the message of which he was the bearer, and as he seems to have been admitted to the conspiracy merely to serve as an escort to the Allobroges, it is probable that he knew few details. Cicero wished to make an immediate impression on the people, and he evidently made it, for, according to Sallust, it was the revelation of a promiscuous conflagration which more than anything else caused the people *mutata mente Catilinae incepta exsecrari.*

The Allobroges were next introduced, and gave evidence on four points. (1) As we know from *pro Sull.* 36, they gave the names of the chief conspirators,[1] probably also keeping back certain names by Cicero's direction, which had been falsely mentioned by Lentulus to inspire confidence (see supr. p. 201). (2) They specified the service which their state was to render, viz. the despatch of some cavalry to Italy. (3) They deposed to the superstitious belief of Lentulus that he was to be the third Cornelius to rule Rome. (4) They testified to the differences of opinion between Cethegus and the rest, the former desiring immediate action, the latter fixing a day amid the Saturnalia. Cicero had already on their previous information sent to the house of Cethegus, and discovered there a quantity of swords and daggers (*in Cat.* iii, 8-10; Plut. *Cic.* 19). There is no indication that the Allobroges supplied any information as to the precise plans of the conspirators in Rome, and even the weapons found with Cethegus might have been for despatch to the army outside. It is true that Cicero specifies the plan, which, according to the Allobroges, was to be postponed to the Saturnalia, as *caedem fieri atque urbem incendi*; but there is the two-fold doubt, (1) whether the Allobroges used these expressions in their evidence; and (2) even if they did, whether their evidence was wholly independent of Cicero's instructions. They were in his power, and the temptation to reinforce Fulvia's story would have been very great.

[1] According to Sallust this disclosure of names was part of the evidence of Volturcius. It may well have come from both sources.

But the most vital part of Cicero's case was to come when the letters taken with the envoys were produced. Cethegus, Statilius, Lentulus and Gabinius, all with varying degrees of readiness, reluctance or truculence, acknowledged their own seals and handwriting. The letters, addressed in each case to the senate and people of the Allobroges, and in identical terms, were compromising, but not damning. Each declared *sese quae eorum legatis confirmasset facturum esse; orare ut item illi facerent quae sibi eorum legati recepissent.* The evidence of Volturcius and of the envoys purported to interpret this ambiguous pledge, and, when we add the letter to Catiline found on Volturcius, which, though unsigned by Lentulus, was fastened by his seal, the presumption of intended and meditated treason was very strong. On the other hand, it does not seem clear that any fresh evidence was produced of urgent and immediate danger of murder and incendiarism in the city. The letters certainly contained no such evidence; the verbal message carried by Volturcius merely spoke vaguely of plans prepared, while if, which is very doubtful, the envoys specified more plainly the nature of these plans, at least they testified to their postponement to the Saturnalia.

But quite apart from Cicero's right, on the strength of the evidence produced, to indulge in sonorous phrases about the destruction of Rome by fire and the massacre of its citizens with their wives and children, it was now proved beyond a doubt that there was a conspiracy in Rome connected with Catiline, an open and declared enemy of the state. It was nevertheless the case that the city was effectively guarded, the authorities on the alert, and, above all, the four chief leaders under arrest.

It was natural and proper that Cicero, having discovered these important proofs of treason, should lay them before the senate, and he had put himself in order by consulting it *de summa republica*, i.e. on the general situation. After hearing the evidence, the senate decreed (1) a vote of thanks to the consul for having saved the state from imminent danger; (2) that Lentulus, having laid down his praetorship, should be kept in safe custody, and also the three others ; (3) that on the ground of Cicero's services a *supplicatio* to the gods should be celebrated, *his verbis*, Cicero says himself, *quod urbem incendiis caede cives Italiam bello liberassem.*[1] As soon as the senate separated, Cicero handed over *in libera custodia* Lentulus to Lentulus Spinther, Cethegus to Cornificius, Statilius to Caesar, Gabinius to Crassus, and Caeparius, now captured, to Terentius. He then in the afternoon of the same day, December 3, addressed the third extant speech to the people, giving a full account of what had so far taken place. The following emphatic declaration confirms, what was implied by the senatorial vote of thanks, the conviction of the responsible authorities that all practical danger was over. *Nunc quoniam, Quirites, consceleratissimi periculo-sissimique belli nefarios duces captos iam et comprehensos tenetis, existimare debetis omnes Catilinae copias, omnes spes atque opes, his depulsis urbis periculis, concidisse* (iii, 16). Catiline alone was formidable, and he only while he was within the city. From Cicero's own showing, therefore, on December 3 the state was already safe from all urgent and immediate danger (1) by the removal of Catiline, (2) by the armed guards protecting the city, (3) and above all, by the arrest of the ringleaders. No doubt the final treatment of these latter would raise serious questions and involve heavy responsibilities, which were clearly filling Cicero with disquiet. *Quodsi omnis impetus domesti-corum hostium depulsus a vobis se in me unum converterit, vobis erit videndum qua conditione posthac eos esse velitis, qui se pro salute vestra obtulerunt invidiae* (iii, 28). But at least it was clear after the senate's decrees and Cicero's public statement that the safety of the republic was no longer involved in the decision, whatever it might be.

But whatever confidence the senate and Cicero might profess, there were still uncertain factors which could not

---

[1] Cicero is quoting to the people from memory. If he quotes correctly, the senate in its excitement must have caught the contagion of Cicero's own balanced style.

wholly be ignored.   What was the attitude of Crassus and Caesar ?   As we have seen, they were probably watching events, with no anxiety as to the result, but ready to take advantage of any false step made by the government. But the meaning of this detached attitude could not have been clear to Cicero or the leading *optimates*.   What they knew was that both leaders had a few years back planned a *coup d'état*, that they had favoured Catiline's claims to the consulship, and that not two months ago they had shown an acquaintance with 'his designs, which, though put on that occasion at the service of the government, was not altogether explained or reassuring.   It is in the light of these considerations, as it seems to me, that we must seek to interpret the statements made by Sallust in cc. 48 and 49.

The day after Cicero's speech to the people was spent by the senate in rewarding the informers and inviting fresh evidence.   The most startling event was the seizure of a man named Tarquinius, said to be on his way from the city to Catiline.   On receiving a promise of pardon, this man not only confirmed what Sallust now says had been the evidence of Volturcius as to plans of murder and incendiarism, but declared that he had a message from Crassus to Catiline, bidding him hasten rather than retard his advance on Rome in consequence of the recent exposure and arrests.

There was great excitement and consternation, some believing, others disbelieving the story, but all agreeing that it was ill-timed and had better be suppressed.   So strong was this feeling that, on Cicero's own proposal, a resolution was passed in the senate, censuring the informa- tion as false, and Tarquinius was thrown into prison. After mentioning an obviously unsatisfactory explanation of the affair as got up by Autronius, Sallust adds that he had himself heard Crassus declare that the affront had been put upon him by Cicero.   There is no indication that Sallust is concerned to defend Crassus, and he expresses no opinion as to the truth of this statement.   That it was actually made by Crassus therefore I can see no reason to doubt. Was it likely to have been true ? If Cicero, as was almost certainly the case, was seriously mistrustful of Crassus, and yet had no evidence against him, the artifice ascribed to him might promise two results. It would create or accentuate suspicion of Crassus among senators, and this would make them more ready to support the extreme measures against the prisoners, which he no doubt, though with some misgivings, contemplated. It would also embarrass Crassus himself, make disloyal action, if any was intended, more difficult, and perhaps prevent Crassus from defending more lenient proposals. These effects would not really be weakened by the quashing of the information, which would not only conceal Cicero's own part in the matter, but might seem to his sensitive but easily satisfied conscience a sufficient reparation for a piece of patriotic dishonesty. It was not an incident which he would include in the history of his consulship, and this perhaps explains why Dio, while mentioning the suspicions against Crassus at this point, and the doubt, belief or disbelief aroused, is silent both about Tarquinius and the decree in the senate (c. 39).

It would seem that a similar view of the situation was taken by some of the leaders of the *optimates*, for Catulus and Piso tried to induce Cicero to have Caesar's name included among those incriminated by the Allobroges. Cicero virtuously refused to do this, realising no doubt that, from his point of view, it was unnecessary, since the suspicion already aroused against Crassus would inevitably extend to Caesar.[1] These *optimates*, however, were not satisfied, but spent this intervening day in spreading fallacious reports as to what Volturcius and the Allobroges had deposed.[2]

[1] If Sallust was anxious, as I believe he was, to keep Caesar out of all suspicion, he should have extended his defence to Crassus, for they were certainly acting together. As it is, he expresses no opinion about Crassus, but says that Cicero refused to allow *ut Caesar falso nominaretur*.

[2] Plutarch (*Cic.* 20) speaks of rumours set afloat by Piso and Silanus.

This was not without effect, for some *equites* on guard outside the temple of Concord showed their *studium in rempublicam* by making threatening demonstrations against Caesar. There can be no doubt that Caesar was the subject of much discussion. Some people, according to Plutarch (c. 20), said that Cicero had his suspicions, but no proof; others that Caesar ἐγγὺς ἐλθὼν ἁλῶναι διεκφύγοι τὸν ἄνδρα; others again that Cicero had proof, but withheld it through fear of Caesar's friends and influence; I have already suggested that Cicero was veiling an allusion, perhaps a warning, to Caesar under what he speaks of as a whole class of Catilinarians, and Plutarch is quite possibly right in stating (*Crass.* 13) that after their death he explicitly charged both Caesar and Crassus with complicity in the conspiracy. At the time they were unknown factors, and this undoubtedly added to the danger and ambiguity of the situation.

By all accounts Cicero was in a state of doubt and anxiety as to what he should do next. The senate had approved his action so far; had accepted the evidence produced as conclusive; and, by ordering the abdication of Lentulus and the incarceration of all arrested, had judged their actions treasonable. *Paulo ante*, says Sallust, *frequens senatus iudicaverat eos contra rempublicam fecisse.* The next step was clearly for the consul, to whom the safety of the state had been entrusted. That the present un-certain position of the prisoners could not be allowed to continue was made clear by an attempt at rescue made by the freedmen and clients of Lentulus and Cethegus. It was suppressed, but as long as the men were confined in the city, it might be repeated (Sall. cc. 49 and 50).

IX

The Decision in the Senate

THERE were practically only two alternatives, since the course adopted with Catiline of allowing him to join the rebel army was no longer admissible. If the safety of the state required it, and if established precedent justified the step, the consul might deal with the prisoners as manifest and confessed *perduelles* and put them summarily to death. If on the other hand this extreme course was not necessary, or not advisable, or of doubtful legality, the consul had the power of transferring the five men from their present informal custody, and of confining them together with the four others, not yet arrested but covered by the senate's decree,[1] under more permanent and regular conditions, until regular judicial proceedings could be taken. Both courses were extraordinary, depended on the condition of martial law supervening on the last decree, and were for the consul, and the consul alone, to decide upon.

Cicero afterwards declared (*ad Att.* xii, 21) that he claimed credit not so much for consulting the senate, as for having made up his mind before he did so : *quod ante quam consulerem iudicaverim,*[2] and I cannot doubt that in his own mind Cicero had decided what course he ought to take, though he knew that it was a course full of danger to himself. No one will deny that Cicero had come to his decision from the most patriotic motives. He had declared in his speech for Rabirius that, if the occasion came, he would act as Marius had acted against Saturninus and his rioters.

---

[1] Cicero (iii, 14) and Sallust (c. 50) agree that the four, whose arrest was decreed, were Cassius Longinus, M. Furius, a colonist of Faesulae, Annius Chilo and Umbrenus.

[2] *Me autem hic* (Brutus) *laudat quod rettulerim, non quod patefecerim, quod cohortatus sim, quod denique ante quam consulerem, ipse iudicaverim. Ad Att.* xii. 21.

He had given these very men fair warning that he would show no mercy, not only to deeds, but to attempts and intentions (*in Cat.* ii, 27). But though Cicero professed himself ready to die for his country with equanimity (iv, 3), in order to take no unnecessary risks he was determined to have the unqualified support of the senate for every step he might take. He therefore summoned that body again on December 5, and laid before it no wider question, but the precise point, *quid de eis fieri placet, qui in custodiam traditi erant* (Sall. c. 50). Though the various decrees of two days before had no meaning unless the prisoners were in the eyes of the senate *damnati*, nevertheless he declares : *ego institui referre ad vos, patres conscripti, tamquam integrum, et de facto quid iudicetis, et de poena quid censeatis* (iv, 6). Cicero's language for the moment is careful and unexceptionable. There was no reason why the senate should not express a *iudicium* on the facts, and indeed it had already done this decisively on the 3rd. Nor was there any reason why senators should not express *sententiae* on the question of punishment, or on any other subject on which a magistrate might ask their advice. But a *iudicium de poena* would have been a dangerous phrase, implying by all its associations a judicial act, possible only for a judicial body, and therefore outside the legal competence of the senate. As a matter of fact, Cicero made little attempt to maintain the nice distinction between *de facto iudicare* and *de poena censere*, and there can be no doubt that, in calling this special meeting of the senate to decide, or even to consider the fate of the prisoners, he came, to say the least of it, within dangerous proximity of violating the *lex Sempronia*. That law prohibited in general terms the setting up of any capital *iudicium* on a Roman citizen except on the authority of the people ; *ne de capite civis Romani iniussu vestrum iudicaretur*. Not only, therefore, was the senate precluded from its former practice of creating special courts independent of *provocatio*, but it was equally precluded from constituting itself as such a court.

Cicero's present action in consulting the senate was ambiguous and capable of more interpretations than one. If he had announced ' I have made up my mind (*iudicavi*) to put these men to death, but before doing so, I should like to hear *quid de poena censeatis*,' or even if he had said ' I should like to hear *quid censeatis* before making up my mind,' Cicero's position, as far as the *lex Sempronia* was concerned, would have been unassailable. The responsibility for the final decision was his alone, but in arriving at it, he was entitled to fortify himself with what advice he chose.

But though the words *quid de facto iudicetis, quid de poena censeatis* were not in themselves inconsistent with this course, the direction and termination given to the debate unquestionably were. Cicero makes it clear throughout his speech that, though the responsibility for acting would be his, and he foresaw the danger involved, the responsibility for the decision to act was to be thrown on to the senate. *Quocunque vestrae mentes atque sententiae inclinant, statuendum vobis ante noctem est.* He leaves no room for doubt that of the two proposals, those of Silanus and of Caesar, he looked to the senate to adopt one or the other, and that his own action would be strictly in accordance with the one which the senate adopted. What he was asking for was not an expression of opinion on the part of leading senators, but a numerical majority in favour of some course of action, which he would then make his own. It is difficult to see how such a vote differed from a judicial pronouncement.

It would seem indeed that Cicero, though he used no technical term implying that the senate was acting as a criminal court, was not unconscious that the *lex Sempronia* might be invoked against him. More than that, the consciousness was brought home to him by a conspicuously vacant seat. The full import of the following highly significant passage is usually overlooked. ' I perceive that among those who claim to be the popular party, a certain person whom I could name is absent. He shrinks,

I imagine, from giving a vote on the life or death of Roman citizens. And yet this same person three days ago handed over Roman citizens into confinement, and decreed a solemn thanksgiving for my services. . . . But he who distributes a prison to the culprit and congratulation to his judge . . . leaves no doubt as to his judgment on the whole case and its merits. But C. Caesar recognises by his presence that the *lex Sempronia* was passed in the interest of Roman citizens; and that enemies of the republic can in no way be regarded as citizens. He remembers too that the very man who passed the Sempronian law, himself paid the extreme penalty to the republic without the authority of the people.'[1]

It is clear from this passage that Cicero knew or suspected that Crassus, the head of the popular party, had absented himself on the ground that to vote in the senate on the life or death of Roman citizens was a violation of the *lex Sempronia*. But though Crassus was absent, Caesar was present, and had even given his *sententia*. The fact suggested to Cicero a highly sophistical and wholly untenable argument. Caesar's presence is an admission that the *lex Sempronia* is not being violated; and this must be because he recognises, what the previous votes of Crassus himself really implied, that the men are not Roman citizens at all, but public enemies, in whose case the senate may, if it chooses, constitute itself a criminal court. Of Caesar's position I shall speak below, but Cicero's argument proves too much, and he characteristically gives away his case by introducing the fate of C. Gracchus. Opimius did not

---

[1] *in Cat.* iv, 10. *Video de istis, qui se populares haberi volunt, abesse nonneminem, ne de capite videlicet civium Romanorum sententiam ferat; is et nudius tertius in custodiam cives Romanos dedit et supplicationem mihi decrevit . . . Iam hoc nemini dubium est, qui reo custodiam quaesitori gratulationem . . . quid de tota re et causa judicaverit. At vero C. Caesar intellegit legem Semproniam esse de civibus Romanis constitutam; qui autem reipublicae sit hostis, eum civem nullo modo esse posse; denique ipsum latorem legis Semproniae iniussu populi poenas reipublicae dependisse.*

violate the *lex Semprònia* when he killed Gracchus *iniussu populi*, because the latter was, or was said to be, an open enemy under arms, whose immediate destruction without trial the safety of the state demanded.   If these men were enemies in the same sense, why did not Cicero take the same course ?   He had said to Catiline *ad mortem te duci iussu consulis iam pridem oportebat*, but he had not executed him, because no manifest and overt act had been committed, and for the same reason he shrank now from taking the extreme and irrevocable step without a judicial or semi-judicial pronouncement on the part of the senate.[1]

That Cicero had really convinced himself that, in spite of the *lex Sempronia*, the senate could in this case pass a sentence of death, is clear from his later declaration that he had only obeyed the senate : *nam relatio illa salutaris et diligens consulis fuerat, animadversio quidem ac iudicium senatus (in Pison.* 7, 14).   On the whole, I cannot resist the conclusion that by this meeting and vote of the senate Cicero rendered himself liable to an impeachment under the *lex Sempronia*, similar to that of Popilius.   As a matter of fact, the threat of impeachment, when it came, took, as we shall see, a different form, because it was deemed more advisable to treat his action as an abuse of the power called into use by the *s. c. ultimum*, and therefore as a violation of the *lex Porcia* or *Valeria*.

For the memorable debate in the senate we have ample evidence, in Sallust (cc. 50 to 53) ; Dio Cassius (cc. 35 and 36) ; Plutarch (*Cic.* 20) ; Appian (ii, 6) ; Suetonius

---

[1] As far as I can see, Cicero regarded the three meetings of the senate, December 3 to 5, as virtually a trial of the prisoners.   On the first the evidence, wholly *ex parte* however, was heard, and the men *damnati* on the facts, as implied by the decrees of this and the second day.   On the third day the sentence was discussed and pronounced.   To confine the term *iudicium* to the question of fact, as distinct from punishment, is specious but untenable, and the distinction is given up in the speech against Piso.   Crassus is criticised for sanctioning the *damnatio* of the first two days, and then protesting against the pronouncement of sentence as contrary to the *lex Sempronia*.

(*Iul.* 14) and Cicero himself. From Sallust we have what purport to be the speeches of Caesar and Cato; from Cicero of course his own speech, very briefly alluded to by Plutarch and Dio, and valuable evidence about Caesar's; while from the later writers and Sallust we gather the general course and order of the debate, a point not altogether ingenuously kept out of sight by Cicero in a passage to be cited below. The general agreement of this evidence is very remarkable, and the few differences of detail quite insignificant. The first senator called upon for his *sententia* was Silanus, consul designate, and he voted *morte multandos esse* (Cic.), *supplicium sumendum* (Sall.), τὴν ἀσχάτην δίκην (Plut. and App.) on the ground that *hoc genus poenae saepe in improbos cives in hac republica esse usurpatum* (*in. Cat.* iv, 7). This opinion was endorsed by Murena, the other consul designate, and by all the prominent consulars, Lutatius Catulus, Torquatus, Cotta, etc. as enumerated by Cicero (*ad Att.* xii, 21).[1] Cicero indeed, followed by Plutarch, declares that all who gave their *sententia* before Caesar, i.e. all of consular rank, gave the same vote. This is, however, disproved by Sallust and Appian, who assert that, before Caesar's turn came, Tiberius Nero proposed that the question should be postponed, the prisoners and the city being in the meantime more strongly guarded : *de ea re, praesidiis additis, referundum* (Sall. c. 50). Appian gives the proposal still more explicitly, that the prisoners should be guarded until Catiline was defeated, and more definite information could be gained. If this is correct, the motion was almost equivalent to the 'previous question' and Cicero perhaps, not regarding it as an independent *sententia*, ignored it. As Sallust declares that, after Caesar's speech, Silanus said that he would support Nero's suggestion, the place which Appian definitely gives it in the debate is confirmed.

It is in any case clear that no formal protest against the

[1] Plutarch places the speech of Catulus after Caesar's, but as he was a consular, we can easily correct this slip.

death penalty was made till Caesar, in his turn as praetor elect, rose to speak. Now Caesar's intervention in the debate cannot be taken to have condoned any violation of the *lex Sempronia*. A sufficiently significant protest on that score had already been made by Crassus, the leader of the popular party, and it was needless and undesirable for that party to be unrepresented in the debate. Besides, if, as is probable, Crassus and Caesar had been waiting for a false move on the part of the government, now was the time for vigilance and alertness. At the same time, Caesar's position was a delicate one. He had every reason to know that suspicions of complicity had been aroused against himself, and might be strengthened if he opposed the course favoured by the majority. But he could not refuse to state his views when called upon by the consul, and those views were bound to be hostile to a new precedent, which would have made more formidable the already dangerous weapon possessed by the senate in its last decree. Accordingly, we find in his speech a protest and a warning combined with a statesmanlike solution of the problem confronting the consul. In proposing the latter, he no doubt knew that it would not be accepted, but its reasonableness and moderation would accentuate the false step on Cicero's part which he foresaw. Summarised from Sallust, his speech was this : ' Let us, as our ancestors did, consult our dignity and not out anger. The latter, looking at the enormity of the crime, might favour this *novum exemplum* ; the former recommends *iis utendum quae legibus comparata sunt.* No punishment is too great for such a crime, but posterity will forget the crime, and remember only the punishment. Besides, if our object is to requite crime by suffering, death is not suffering, but release from it. Why not then let scourging precede death ? Do you say that would violate the *lex Porcia* ? Yes ; but, if it comes to that, so would the infliction of death. Is it safe to respect the law in the lighter matter and to neglect it in the heavier ? The proposal of Silanus *aliena a nostra republica videtur.* New precedents, even directed *in parricidas reipublicae*, are dangerous. History shows that they never stand still. Do not sanction a precedent which, justified perhaps now and in the present consul's hands, may recoil upon us in the future and in less scrupulous hands. Our ancestors, who passed the *lex Porcia* and other laws allowing even condemned criminals to escape death by exile, were wiser than we. I urge you not to violate those laws. At the same time, to prevent these men from joining Catiline, I suggest that their goods should be taken possession of by the consul ; that they themselves should be confined in towns selected for their wealth [1] ; that a heavy fine should be imposed on any such town which allows a prisoner to escape ; and that any proposal to senate or people modifying these acts should be declared treason to the state.'

The chief points in the speech are : (1) the disavowal of all sympathy with the prisoners ; (2) the ignoring of Cicero's precedents, and the insistence that a *novum exemplum* is involved. In former cases there had been some overt act ; here there was nothing but evidence of intention to go upon, and in future cases, if not in this, *potest falsum aliquid pro vero credi* ; (3) the veiled warning contained in the reference to the *lex Porcia* ; and (4) the nature and meaning of the actual *sententia*.

This last must be regarded as merely Caesar's advice to the consul in answer to his appeal for advice. It was not, as Cicero affects to understand it, the proposal of a punishment alternative to, and even severer than, that of Silanus. If Cicero chose to put it to the vote as such, that was his affair. It merely suggested certain immediate measures of precaution, which the consul, and the consul alone, might take on the strength of the last decree. If

[1] Sall. c. 51. The argument, though not the style, is Caesarian, and probably authentic. Dio and Plutarch both insist on its appearance of moderation and equity. The point about the fine on *municipia* comes from Cicero (iv, 8) and is confirmed by Dio (c. 36). Several minor points in Sallust's version also receive confirmation from Cicero, especially the remarks on the subject of death.

the men had property, which was perhaps doubtful, it was wise to impound it, lest it should help the rebels or secure their own release. It was a matter for the consul, certainly not for the senate, and, as a matter of fact, Cicero on his own authority refrained from confiscation after the execution (Plut. *Cic.* 21).

With regard to the custody of the prisoners, the present ἄδεσμος φυλακή was a momentary expedient, and some more definite and secure mode of confinement was clearly a necessity. The retention of the men in Rome would be a possible cause of disturbance, while in orderly towns of Italy they could be kept safe, and would be no danger.[1] Cicero suggests that it was unfair to impose such a burden on Italian towns, but according to Sallust's *mos Romanus* (c. 29) the consul, acting under the *s. c. ultimum*, was entitled *coercere omnibus modis socios atque cives*,[2] and the order would be of course provisional on the continuance of the crisis. Cicero's contention that Caesar was proposing a sentence of perpetual imprisonment is ridiculous. *Itaque homo mitissimus atque lenissimus non dubitat P. Lentulum aeternis tenebris vinculisque mandare, et sancit in posterum, ne quis huius supplicio levando se iactare et in perniciem populi Romani posthac popularis esse possit* (iv, 10). But Plutarch and Appian make perfectly clear, what the speech in Sallust also implies, that the confinement was primarily intended to prevent the men from joining Catiline, and was therefore only to last ἄχρι ἂν οὗ καταπολεμωθῇ Κατιλείνας (Plut. c. 21). It would also be possible in this way either to institute an impeachment for *perduellio*, or to cause an accusation to be brought under the *lex Plautia*, as was actually done in the case of the lesser conspirators in the following year. Caesar may not have specified this

[1] The richest towns would be selected, because those suffering from *aes alienum* might be suspected of sharing the *novarum rerum studium*.

[2] Where Sallust speaks of *socios atque cives*, I have no doubt that he gives to *socios* its old connotation of Italians as distinct from Romans.

object, for it was not his business, but it must have been obvious to all, and Appian no doubt had authority for saying μέχρι ἂν Κατιλείνα καταπολεμωθέντος ἐπὶ δικαστήριον ἀπαχθῶσι. Cicero apparently based his phrase *sempiterna vincula* on Caesar's *sanctio* that no proposal for release to senate or people should be permissible. But such a *sanctio* was a very usual precaution, and generally a futile one, against the reversal of some act or measure. As long as martial law was maintained, i.e. till the end of the crisis, this might have been enforced, but no longer. It is strange that a theory of life-long imprisonment, nowhere else even hinted at, should have grown up out of Cicero's obviously rhetorical phrases *aeternis tenebris* and *sempiterna vincula*.

This speech, coming from a man so influential and representative as Caesar, made a deep impression on the senate. Those who spoke next, either from conviction or apprehension or consideration for Cicero's safety,[1] opposed the death penalty, while some, if not most of the previous speakers, withdrew their *sententiae*, Silanus in particular declaring that he should now support the postponement suggested by Nero.[2]

It was at this point that Cicero intervened, not with a

[1] Plutarch puts the eagerness of Cicero's friends to adopt Caesar's proposal after Cicero's own speech, and makes even Silanus change his mind at this point. But Cicero's opening sentences show that his friends had already manifested their anxiety on his account, and it can hardly be doubted that Sallust is right in attributing Silanus' change of view to Caesar's speech. I suspect that we have not Cicero's speech exactly as it was delivered. He could hardly have ignored completely the retreat of Silanus, though, as the latter came round again after Cato's speech, there was no need in the edited version to allude to a regrettable incident. For the same reason it is kept out of sight in the letter to Atticus referred to.

[2] Suetonius (c. 14) and Plutarch say that Silanus was led to give a non-natural interpretation to his own proposal, explaining, according to the latter, that ἐσχάτη δίκη in the case of senators could mean no more than imprisonment. This does not deserve to be set against the statement of Sallust: *permotus oratione Caesaris pedibus in sententiam Ti. Neronis iturum se dixerat, qui de ea re, praesidiis additis, referundum censuerat.*

sententia, but to straighten out the issues, and, as it seems to me, to undo the effects of Caesar's speech.

' Do not think of my safety ; decide in the interests of the state. I am accustomed to danger, and I am ready to face death. What did the Gracchi or Saturninus do comparable with what these men intended—the burning of the city, the murder of you all, the admission of Catiline into Rome, the tempting of the Allobroges, the summons to slaves ? You have had their own letters and confessions, and you marked your belief in their guilt by your decrees of two days ago. Nevertheless I put the case before you, and ask for your decision as to the punishment. Remember that the danger is not confined to the city ; it has spread through Italy and even reached the provinces. Two proposals are before you, that of Silanus for death, and that of Caesar for perpetual imprisonment and confiscation of property. I see where my own interest lies. If I have to carry out the proposal of a popular leader, I shall be safe from popular attacks, but if the other, I foresee trouble. Nor is Caesar's proposal more lenient ; it is even more severe. It takes away all that life is worth, but withholds death, the end of misery. But have we any right to be merciful except to the state ? Think of what was to happen—yourselves murdered, the citizens exterminated, the city in ashes, Gauls installed on its ruins, Italy devastated, no one left even to mourn the name of the republic. The danger is, not that we may be too severe, but that we may be too lenient. All classes are ready to support you, but they expect safety in return. *Obsessa facibus et telis impiae coniurationis vobis supplex manus tendit patria. It is for you to protect all that una nox paene delevit.*'

Plutarch (c. 21) describes Cicero as making an ambiguous speech, τὰ μὲν τῇ προτέρᾳ τὰ δὲ τῇ γνώμῃ Καίσαρος συνειπών, and there was certainly a note of wobbling about it. But though he praised Caesar's attitude, it was the faint praise which damns, and his grotesquely exaggerated picture, utterly unjustified by the evidence which he had produced, can only have been intended to drive the senate into the severest course.   In effect, what Dio says is true : καί σφας συνταράξας τε καὶ ἐκφοβήσας ἔπεισε θάνατον τῶν συνειλημμένων καταγνῶναι (xxxvii, 35).

But whatever the effect produced by Cicero's speech, that of Cato, who followed, speaking as tribune elect, decided the prisoners' fate.   Plutarch (*Cat. min.* 23) states that Cato's speech was taken down at the time, and, if so, Sallust no doubt followed its general lines.

'When war is threatening all that we hold dear, prevention rather than punishment is needed, and to wait for overt acts is to be too late both for safety and for punishment.   I have often upbraided you for luxury and avarice, and though you disregarded me, the republic survived.   Now it is a question of life or death, of freedom or slavery.   However we misuse words, let us not spare those who seek our blood, and call it mercy.   We need not decide whether death is the end of trouble, or, for wretches like these, the beginning of torture.   But when Caesar suggests imprisonment in Italian towns, he presumably fears rescue in Rome.   There is the same risk outside Rome, and less means of preventing it.   Or if he alone is not touched by the general fear, then indeed we should look to ourselves.   Remember that, in deciding on the fate of these men, you are deciding the fate of Catiline's army.   You have lost your old virtues, and what is the result ?   Here are men who have conspired to burn their country, and have roused Gauls to war ; there is an armed leader with an army ;   and yet you hesitate to punish enemies captured within the walls.   You wait for one another ; you hope the gods will save the state.   If there were any redeeming feature about the men you think of sparing, it might be different, but there is none. There is not a moment to lose.   Catiline's army is at our throats, and, with enemies within, all our plans are known. My vote therefore is, since the state is in urgent danger, and these men are proved on the evidence of Volturcius and the Allobroges to have planned murder and incendiarism, that *de confessis, sicuti manifestis rerum capitalium, more maiorum supplicium sumendum.*'

As Plutarch and Appian elaborate the point that Cato drew marked attention to the suspicions against Caesar, it is probable that Sallust has toned down this feature of the speech. Cato virtually admits that there had been no overt act on the part of the prisoners, but there was evidence of intention in conjunction with open enemies, and, in order to save the state against the latter danger, they must be dealt with *sicuti manifesti rerum capitalium*, i.e. on the presumption that they were *perduelles*.

After this speech there was a decisive revulsion of feeling towards the more drastic course, but Cicero, discarding the *sententiae* of the consulars who had vacillated, chose Cato's proposal to put to the vote. This was not unnatural, but years after Cicero was highly indignant at the suggestion that he had put Cato's proposal to the vote because it was the first proposal of the death penalty. It only put in clearer terms what all the consulars had voted before (*ad Att.* xii, 21). This is true, but it is significant that in this passage, which is sometimes relied on as giving the best account of the order of debate, Cicero keeps back the fact that most of the consulars had withdrawn their *sententiae*, or would not, prior to Cato's speech, have been prepared to stand by them.[1] The senate adopted Cato's *sententia*, and Cicero immediately acted upon it. On the same day, to prevent possible disturbances during the night, he led the five prisoners to the *carcer*, and caused them to be strangled; announcing on his way back to the waiting crowds in the forum that all of them were dead.

[1] Cicero mentions as the consulars who had voted for death, Catulus, Servilius, the Luculli, Curio, Torquatus, Lepidus, Volcacius, Figulus, Cotta, L. Caesar, C. Piso, Silanus and Murena.

X

The Attitude of Caesar and Metellus Nepos

THAT the five men richly deserved their fate no one will deny now, and Caesar did not deny then. It is an insult to C. Gracchus and even to Saturninus to weigh their acts against the designs of these degraded and despicable types of Roman revolutionaries. When Gracchus allowed himself to head an armed sedition, Opimius, responding to the exhortation of the senate, had risked a new precedent ; and the people subsequently had justified his action and sanctioned that precedent. It is by no means impossible that it would have sanctioned a modification and extension of that precedent to meet the present case, if it had been called upon to decide. But at the time, as we shall see, no opportunity was given to the people to confirm or condemn, and when, some years later, there might have been an opportunity, Cicero shrank from facing it, and let judgment go against him by default.

As it was, politically and legally, the government, represented officially by Cicero, had perhaps made the false step for which the popular leaders had been presumably on the watch. They were not, as it turned out, able at the moment to make full use of it, but Caesar, aided by Metellus Nepos, made the attempt.

I have already argued that, whether Cicero's reference to the senate was or was not a violation of the *lex Sempronia*, this was not made the point of attack. The glaring fact of the execution threw into the shade the question of criminal court or no criminal court ; for there certainly had been no appeal, and therefore on the face of it the *lex Porcia* had been violated, which, like the earlier Valerian laws, prohibited the death penalty without *provocatio*. It was obviously no adequate defence to say that the senate had passed its last decree; *darent operam consules ne quid respublica detrimenti caperet*. That in itself was neither an order nor even a permission to break a fundamental law. It was merely an exhortation to save the state from enemies. It was for the consul to interpret the exhortation, and, unless there was a precedent established by custom or law, he did so at his own risk. Opimius had to take this risk in 121, but his acquittal by a *iudicium populi* confirmed and established his interpretation as a *mos Romanus*. From that time it was not questioned that, when on the senate's exhortation the consul had ' called the people to arms ' against acts of overt war, violence or murder on the part of the citizens, he might, to save the state, kill them in fight, or take them to the *carcer* and execute them, the *lex Porcia* being in temporary suspension. On the present occasion the last decree had been passed, but primarily to meet the danger from the rebel army headed by Manlius, and soon by Catiline. It justified Cicero's extraordinary action in raising and sending out armed levies under Celer, Antonius and others ; it justified acts of war in Italy ; and, if Catiline had been captured, it would unquestionably have justified his summary execution. But with regard to the conspirators left behind in Rome, the case was not so simple. Partly by the good offices of Crassus and Caesar, partly through good fortune, partly through information supplied by his own agents, Cicero had a certain amount of evidence, the evidence of Fulvia, Volturcius and the Gallic envoys. He had also, and both he and Cato made much of the fact, the ' confessions ' of Lentulus and his companions. But on Cicero's own showing in the speech of December 3 it is clear that these merely amounted to the acknowledgment of their own letters, and involved no admission of their designs within the city. The evidence was by no means all of it unimpeachable, but we may take it as proving the existence of plans for murder, incendiarism and treason with a Gallic tribe, as well as of co-operation with Catiline. That undoubtedly constituted the men enemies of the state in intention, by presumption, and on the strength of statements not judicially tested. It abundantly justified arrest, in order to prevent these intentions from becoming overt acts. But it did not constitute the prisoners manifest and overt enemies, only to be dealt with by sword in hand or by instant execution. The case was obviously not covered by established precedent ; and to act, notwithstanding this, as Opimius and Marius had acted, was therefore, as Caesar contended, a *novum exemplum.* It was a procedure based, not on manifest acts, but on inference from evidence, which, even if true in the present instance, might be false in future cases ; *potest falsum aliquid pro vero credi.* It was therefore an unsanctioned violation of the *lex Porcia.* This, if I understand it rightly, was the position of Caesar, and is to be detected in his speech. Cicero does not meet these points ; he ignores the objection that he is introducing a *novum exemplum,* he thinks it enough to urge the gravity and enormity of the danger involved in the designs which he had exposed and stopped. In doing this, he signally illustrates Caesar's warning as to the possible misuse of evidence ; for he scandalously and unblushingly exaggerates and misrepresents it. He had produced evidence that there were plans of incendiarism in the city ; he describes it as *totius urbis incendium,* or *incendium patriae.* He had produced evidence that many persons were to be murdered ; he speaks of it as a universal massacre of men, women and children, so complete that no one would be left to mourn the name of Rome. He had evidence that, in return for concessions in the matter of debt, the Allobroges were to supply Catiline with cavalry ; he describes a plot for installing Gauls on the ashes of Rome. Cicero employed these ' terminological inexactitudes ' so often that he perhaps came to believe that they were true ; but the most elementary tests for weighing evidence show that at least the charges were not proved.

Still, if the execution of these five men on the ground of complicity with Catiline was really necessary to save the state, Cicero only did his duty in risking a *novum exemplum*, which he might have justified to the people afterwards, as Opimius had done. Perhaps the burning and the massacres might still be carried out, if the five leaders were left alive. But the city was hedged round with the consul's guards ; the populace, incensed at the designs revealed, was on the *qui vive*; the leaders, already in safe keeping, might, if Caesar's advice was followed, be securely guarded out of reach of Rome till the crisis was over. As far as the internal conspiracy was concerned, the state was already saved. Cicero triumphantly proclaimed this both now and afterwards ; the senate officially recognised it by the vote of thanks, and the decree of a *supplicatio*, on the express ground that he had saved the republic.

A less illogical position was taken up by Cato. For him the state was still in danger, but not from inside Rome. ' The army of Catiline is at our throats ; make an example of these miscreants, and it will dissolve away ; show signs of weakness, and it will overwhelm us.' But Cicero knew, if Cato did not, that Catiline's army was never a serious danger. Catiline was only a danger inside the walls. The consul had almost driven him to join the army, and was only anxious because the other conspirators had not joined it too. He had contemptuously compared it with his own forces, and he had told the people on December 3 that with the disclosure of the plot in Rome, and the arrest of the leaders, the whole strength and hope of Catiline had collapsed. It is sometimes assumed that Cato is proved to have been right by the following passage of Sallust : *postquam in castra nuntius pervenit Romae coniurationem patefactam, de Lentulo et Cethego ceterisque . . . supplicium sumptum, plerique quos ad bellum spes rapinarum aut novarum rerum studium inlexerat, dilabuntur*. But it is obvious that not terror of punishment, but conviction of failure caused the dispersal, and this was due to the disclosure and arrest. Not Cato's prediction but Cicero's boast receives verification from Sallust's statement (c. 57). When Catiline left Rome on

November 7, he apparently contemplated a rapid swoop on the city, where the authorities were to be distracted by the simultaneous rising from within. But he found that the army of Manlius amounted to no more than 2,000 half-armed men (Sall. c. 56). During the next three weeks he succeeded in raising his numbers to two full legions, perhaps 12,000 men, of whom, however, only one-fourth part was equipped with military arms.[1] He might no doubt have swelled his numbers with slaves from the *ergastula*, but this, in spite of the exhortations of Lentulus, he refused to do. Meanwhile his chance was lost, for Metellus Celer soon had three legions in Picenum, while Antonius was advancing from the south with a still larger force. All that remained was to manœuvre hither and thither in the mountains, hoping, according to Sallust, for considerable reinforcements on news arriving of a successful *coup* in Rome. If this was so, there must have been hopeless misunderstanding, for the conspirators were waiting according to agreement for Catiline to strike. At any rate, after December 5 his half-armed army began to melt away. With what remained, about 3,000 men, he attempted to withdraw towards Gaul, but finding that Metellus had turned his position by intercepting his descent from the mountains, and that Antonius was hemming him in on the south, he turned desperately on the latter and was destroyed with his whole army in the early days of January.[2]

But during the last weeks of December people in Rome troubled themselves little about Catiline's fate. The whole conspiracy had flickered out with the public exposure and arrest on the 3rd, and after the striking events of the 5th, Cicero was perhaps for the moment the hero of the hour. But the very suddenness of the collapse must have made the public soon realise that the whole affair had been

[1] Appian says 20,000, but agrees as to the proportion of unarmed.

[2] Sallust's concluding chapters sufficiently explain the military situation.

unduly magnified, and probably Dio's judgment represents
the more sober views of the time : καὶ ἐπὶ πλεῖόν γε τῆς
τῶν πραχθέντων ἀξίας ὄνομα πρὸς τὴν τοῦ Κικέρωνος δόξαν καὶ
πρὸς τοὺς λόγους τοὺς κατ᾽ αὐτοῦ λεχθέντας ἔσχε (c. 42).

Undoubtedly Cicero had increased his reputation. Once
put upon the right track by Crassus, and aided by some
good fortune, he had taken adequate precautions, and
carried the affair through with steadiness and judgment.
He had no doubt persuaded himself that the state was in
real and imminent danger, and he had accepted what he
knew to be considerable personal risk (*mei capitis periculi*)
in his final act. He was almost certainly suspicious of the
part played by Crassus and Caesar[1] in spite of the warnings
received by them, but he was painfully conscious that
they were not materially affected by the collapse of the
conspiracy. He probably regretted Cato's innuendos in
the senate, and he must have been embarrassed by the
behaviour of the extreme *optimates* as well as of some of the
equites.

[1] It can hardly be doubted that both Crassus and Caesar were
suspected by the *optimates* generally of being somehow concerned
in the conspiracy. This was the result, not wholly unnatural, of
their former connexion with Catiline and of their marked reserve
during the whole affair. The existence of the suspicion against
Crassus is explicitly stated by Sallust and Dio ; that against
Caesar comes out in the action of Catulus and Piso, in the speech
of Cato, in the hostile demonstration of the *equites*, and in the
episode of Curius and Vettius. Cicero himself was most careful
not to countenance this suspicion, but he was of course aware of
it, and he certainly shared it. There is no reason to doubt the
statement of Plutarch (*Crassus* 13) that in a work published after
Caesar's death Cicero φανερὸς ἦν Κράσσῳ καὶ Καίσαρι τὴν αἰτίαν
προστριβόμενος. That Crassus found it diplomatic early in 61
to expatiate on Cicero's services in having saved the state was
not likely to have removed these suspicions, though Cicero naturally makes the most of it in a letter to Atticus (i, 14, 3). It is
amusing to note the puzzled complacency with which Cicero
listened to his own familiar outpourings about flames and murder
seriously repeated by Crassus : *totum hunc locum quem ego varie
nostris orationibus . . . soleo pingere, de flammis, de ferro,
nosti illas* ληκύθους, *valde graviter pertexuit.*

According to authorities used by Plutarch (*Caes.* 7), the latter needed only a sign from Cicero to attack Caesar as he left the senate after the debate on the 5th. The story may be true, notwithstanding Cicero's silence as to the incident in his history of his consulship.[1] Still more awkward were the disclosures of Vettius, almost certainly prompted by men like Catulus and Piso. Dio (c. 41) gives a vague account of the reckless charges brought by this informer, but Suetonius (*Iul.* 17) declares that he made special charges against Caesar, offering to produce a letter written by him to Catiline. As Curius made similar charges in the senate, Caesar thought it worth while publicly to call upon Cicero to say whether he had or had not received from him certain information concerning the conspiracy. Cicero acknowledged that this was the case, and Vettius and Curius were discredited. The incident was the occasion for a popular demonstration, which proved that Caesar's reserved attitude during the crisis had increased rather than diminished his influence with the populace. According to Plutarch the crowd, knowing what was on foot, waited outside the senate till Caesar appeared in safety, while, if Suetonius is to be believed, Vettius narrowly escaped being torn in pieces in the forum.

The course of events indeed on the whole had turned out not unfavourably to the popular leaders. If they had lost a once useful agent in Catiline, at least his mad and furious schemes of revolution had been disposed of without serious compromise to the popular party or its programme. The senatorial party had scored an administrative success, but this was as likely to be displeasing to Pompey as to themselves, and, on the supposition of some understanding with him, its effect could be no more than temporary. But even the temporary triumph might be marred by the questionable step which Cicero

---

[1] It is exactly the sort of incident which Cicero might be expected to omit. On the other hand, it is curiously like the incident placed by Sallust between December 3 and 5.

had taken on the authority of the senatorial government. Caesar, when called upon, had given honest and
straightforward advice, based on common sense and not
inconsistent with constitutional precedent. But from the
point of view of his own interests he must have felt some
satisfaction at seeing it disregarded. That Caesar must
have been keenly on the alert for any false move in the
delicate matter of giving due, and not more than due,
effect to the senate's last decree, is to my mind placed
beyond doubt by the episode not many months before
of the Rabirian impeachment. Caesar would himself
keep in the background, as he had done throughout the
year, but Metellus Nepos, who would become tribune on
December 10th, was, it would seem, told off to prepare the
popular mind for what might happen. While the trial
of Murena was still going on, Metellus was making in-
flammatory speeches of some kind to the people. *In
hesterna contione intonuit vox perniciosa tribuni designati*
(*pro Mur.* 31), and it seems impossible not to connect these
attacks of Metellus with the repeated references in Cicero's
two last speeches to the personal danger which threatened
himself. That as soon as the tribunes entered on their
office, Cicero was made the object of deliberate attack on
the ground of the executions, is as clear from his own
admissions as from the statements of Plutarch and Dio
Cassius. The former (c. 23) associates Bestia [1] with
Metellus, and suggests that both were acting with Caesar.
Dio Cassius (c. 42) says: Κικέρων δὲ ὀλίγου μὲν καὶ παραχρῆμα
ἐπὶ τῇ τοῦ Λεντούλου τῶν τε ἄλλων τῶν δεθέντων σφαγῇ ἐκρίθη·
Τὸ δὲ ἔγκλημα τοῦτο λόγῳ μὲν ἐκείνῳ ἐπεφέρετο, ἔργῳ δὲ ἐπὶ τῇ
βουλῇ κατεσκευάζετο. Ὡς γὰρ οὐκ ἐξόν σφισιν ἄνευ τοῦ δήμου
θάνατον πολίτου τινὸς καταψηφίσασθαι, πολλὴν καταβοὴν ἐν τῷ
ὁμίλῳ πρὸς τοῦ Μετέλλου τοῦ Νέπωτος ὅτι μάλιστα εἶχον.

---

[1] It is probable that Bestia took part with Metellus in the agitation against Cicero. Though Metellus had certainly left Rome
before the *pro Sull.* was delivered, there was still one tribune left
ad lugendos coniuratos (41). This is generally referred to Bestia,
and, I think, rightly.

It was plainly the intention of Metellus to impeach Cicero as soon as he laid down the consulship. Having this intention, he naturally took care that Cicero should not use the occasion of laying down office on December 31 for another oratorical display. Several days before the end of the year, he declared in a *contio : ei qui in alios animadvertisset indicta causa, dicendi ipsi potestatem fieri non oportere.*[1] Accordingly, when the day came, Metellus vetoed all but the formal oath of abdication, and though Cicero added to this an oath that he had saved the republic, it is not certain that this was received as enthusiastically as he himself declares.[2] At any rate, three days later, *a.d. iii Non. Ian.*, Metellus again violently attacked Cicero, aiming at his overthrow, *consilio animoque inimicissimo.* But the senate felt itself strong enough to intervene with effect against the threatened impeachment, passing a decree of indemnity in favour of all who had taken part in the recent measures, and declaring that an impeachment would be regarded as the act of an enemy. οὐ μὴν καὶ ὦφλε τότε οὐδέν τῆς γὰρ γερουσίας ἄδειαν πᾶσι τοῖς διαχειρίσασι τὰ τότε πραχθέντα δούσης, καὶ προσέτι καὶ προσειπούσης ὅτι, κἂν αὖθίς τις εὐθῦναί τινα αὐτῶν τολμήσῃ, ἔν τε ἐχθροῦ καὶ ἐν πολεμίου μοίρᾳ ἔσται, ἐφοβήθη τε ὁ Νέπως καὶ οὐδὲν ἔτ' ἐκίνησεν (D. C. c. 42). As an impeachment was certainly threatened and as certainly dropped, this statement of Dio probably rests on good authority. Caesar no doubt thought it better to proceed with caution. An impeachment of Cicero might wait, and would always be a useful party move.

But I have assumed, so far on grounds of general probability, that the comparative indifference of Caesar and

---

[1] *ad fam.* v, 2, 8. Cicero gives his version of the action of Nepos in a letter to his brother Metellus Celer. He also speaks in *pro Sest.* 5, 12 of the new tribunes *qui tum extremis diebus consulatus mei res eas quas gesseram vexare cupiebant.*

[2] Dio at least (c. 38) says that the act made him more hated than before. Metellus no doubt deprived us of a fine piece of oratory, but passages in *pro Sull.*, e.g. 33, give us specimens of what we should have had.

Crassus to the situation in Rome during the latter part
of the year was due to the prospect of better relations with
Pompey, and that these were to be brought about through
the intermediation of Metellus Nepos, who had come from
Pompey's camp for the tribunician elections in the early
summer. That in sending home Metellus, Pompey had
no idea of a *rapprochement* with the senatorial party, is
clear from the haste with which Cato was put up to oppose
him. That Metellus was to have acted alone in Pompey's
interest against both *optimates* and popular leaders, it is
impossible to believe. On the other hand, an agreement
of some kind between Pompey and the popular leaders
would clear the horizon for the latter, while for the former
it would render unnecessary some very decisive and
critical action at no distant date. But while it may be
claimed for this hypothesis that it explains better than
any other the singular aloofness and unconcern maintained by Caesar and Crassus during the exciting months
between July and December, it undoubtedly needs some
more concrete verification.

In my opinion it receives this from the incidents at the
beginning of 62, as recorded by Suetonius and Dio Cassius
(Suet. *Iul.* 15 and 16; D. C. xxxvii, 43). According to
these authorities combined, on the very first day of his
praetorship Caesar gave notice of a law for transferring
the honour of completing the Capitoline temple from
Lutatius Catulus to Pompey. The date, explicitly vouched
for by Suetonius, made what was clearly meant for a
manifesto more impressive.[1] The proposal encountered
the most violent opposition from the senatorial party,
and, having served its purpose as a manifesto to Pompey,
and having compelled the *optimates* to show their hand,
it was dropped. Dio regards Caesar's motive as the mere

---

[1] Suetonius does not mention Pompey's name in the matter,
but this is convincingly supplied by Dio. Dio only mentions
the incident after the withdrawal of Metellus, but his language
implies that its relinquishment and not its inception belongs to
this point.

desire to win popularity by honouring Pompey, the hero of the populace. But Pompey had been even more the hero of the people a year earlier, and yet Caesar had not hesitated to defy him in the Rullan proposal. I see no way of explaining the affair except as an indication of completely changed relations between the two men.

This is equally brought out if we piece together the evidence of Dio and Suetonius as to the co-operation of Caesar and Metellus Nepos in another stirring series of incidents early in the year.[1] Suetonius states that Caesar came forward as the confederate and champion of Metellus in trying to carry certain turbulent laws. What the main law was, we gather from Dio and Plutarch. Its object was to recall Pompey from the East, with the view of re-establishing order in the state (τοῦ τὰ παρόντα κατασταθῆναι, Dio). On the other hand, Plutarch suggests a somewhat different motive : καὶ νόμος ὑπ᾽ αὐτῶν (Caesar and Metellus) εἰσήγετο καλεῖν Πομπήϊον μετὰ τῆς στρατιᾶς, ὡς δὴ καταλύσοντα τὴν Κικέρωνος δυναστείαν (c. 23). The real meaning of this scheme seems to me unmistakable.[2] It was the first formal step towards establishing that coalition between the opponents of senatorial government which, in the complicated situation grown up since 67, could alone prevent something like optimatist supremacy in the present, and civil war in the future. It is difficult to believe that it was a scheme only thought out in January 62 ; it was far more likely the basis of an understanding arrived at six months earlier, when Metellus had first come from the East as Pompey's emissary. The latter's work was then approaching com-

[1] Plutarch confirms Suetonius as to the joint action of Metellus and Caesar. Dio omits the part played by Caesar, but he implies it when he remarks that after the retirement of Metellus, οὐδ᾽ ὁ Καῖσαρ . . . ἔτ᾽ ἐνεωτέρισεν.

[2] I can find no indication in the authorities that the idea of recalling Pompey had ever had any connexion with putting down the conspiracy. When Metellus came home there was no conspiracy, and when this law was proposed the conspiracy was a thing of the past.

pletion, and, in view of the strong senatorial position, threatening equally to Pompey and to the two leaders at home, it may well have seemed conducive to the interests of all for Pompey to come home next year, with his position legitimised by a popular summons. What use should be made of the army might be left for events to decide. The programme was not at this time carried out, and we do not know how ' order ' would have been ' restored,' but that there would have been an end to the δυναστεία of Cicero, or more correctly of the senate, we may be sure.

How much of this Cicero had foreseen or suspected, when in his speech for Murena he pointed out the dangers of the coming year and the necessity of having two dependable consuls, is not certain. But it looks as if Caesar had underrated the confidence and consequent strength of the senate, resulting from the series of small successes scored during the recent years, and culminating in the collapse of the conspiracy. In spite of his support, the opposition of Cato and other tribunes blocked the law, and, though Metellus was as pertinacious as Cornelius had been in 67 under similar conditions, the matter resolved itself into street fighting. Once more the senate, encouraged no doubt by the recent failure to impeach Cicero, passed the last decree. καὶ τά τε ἱμάτια ἠλλάξαντο καὶ τοῖς ὑπάτοις τὴν φυλακὴν τῆς πόλεως ὥστε μηδὲν ἀπ' αὐτῆς ἀποτριβῆναι ἐπέτρεψαν. This practically had the effect of suspending Metellus from his duties as tribune, while, if Suetonius is right in saying that Caesar too was suspended from his judicial office, the consuls must have supplemented the senate's decree by the proclamation of a *iustitium*. Caesar, not being prepared now for the *coup d'état* which he had contemplated some years earlier, allowed his new policy to remain for the moment in abeyance, making a show of submission and refusing the popular support offered him. Metellus on his part, after issuing a public protest, left Italy to report to Pompey what had happened.

Whatever Cicero's real suspicions may have been, he still tried to persuade himself and others that Caesar and

Crassus were jealous of Pompey's successes and appre-
hensive of his intentions. He even tried to impress this
upon Pompey himself. *Sed hoc scito, tuos veteres hostes,
novos amicos, vehementer literis perculsos atque ex magna
spe deturbatos iacere.*[1] If my view of the situation is
correct, this was a delusion on Cicero's part. The popular
leaders were probably reassured as to Pompey's intentions,
and could therefore afford to acquiesce in the *status quo*
for the present. If so, it was doubtless arranged through
Metellus that it was advisable not to precipitate matters
by Pompey's immediate return.

Meanwhile in official circles there was a great show of
upholding Cicero's action, and much activity was displayed
in the prosecution of Autronius, Vargunteius and other
conspirators, most of whom were condemned in absence
(*pro Sull.* 6 and 7; conf. 92; D. C. c. 41). Cicero had
himself given evidence against these men, but he was
thankful for the chance of defending Sulla, as a set off
against his previous severity, and, in spite of sonorous
reassertions of his unparalleled services, he shows himself
throughout the speech keenly conscious of his position :
*quare non nescius sum quanto periculo vivam in tanta
multitudine improborum* (*pro Sull.* 28). Cicero is indeed
surprised that his opponent, Torquatus, should doubt the
popular approval of the executions, but the hints dropped
de supplicio, de laqueo, de carcere were not without significance and menace. But even more disquieting perhaps
than hints and threats at home was Pompey's ominous
silence. *Eas res gessi,* Cicero writes to Pompey, *quarum
aliquam in tuis literis . . . gratulationem expectavi*
(*ad fam.* v, 7). But Pompey made no sign of approval
or sympathy.

I do not propose to carry this enquiry beyond the immediate situation supervening on the collapse of Catiline's
conspiracy, only noting as a further indication of an

---

[1] *ad fam.* v, 7, written in April 62. I understand the phrases
veteres hostes and *novos amicos* to refer to Caesar and Crassus before
and after the understanding through Metellus.

understanding between Pompey and the popular leaders at home, the postponement of the consular elections in order that M. Piso, a lieutenant of Pompey, might arrive in time to stand. Dio Cassius (c. 44) vaguely says that this was because οὕτω πάντες τὸν Πομπήιον ἔδεισαν. But though Cicero's own attitude towards Pompey was conciliatory, that of the *optimates* was uncompromisingly hostile, and it is impossible not to detect in this episode the influence of Crassus and Caesar. What I desire to suggest as a clue for understanding the position of Caesar during the year 63 is his far-sighted conviction that the ultimate solution of the political situation was to be found in a coalition of himself and Crassus with Pompey. This conviction seems to me to date from the end of 64, and to explain the underlying motive for the huge scheme of land purchase in the Rullan proposal, by which a favourable basis of negotiations with Pompey would have been provided. When this attempt to meet future eventualities was frustrated, I believe that actual negotiations were opened up with Pompey, and that their existence gives us the best explanation of the apparently indifferent and detached position of the two leaders during the second half of 63. Finally, I suspect that Pompey's resignation of his military command and his retirement into a private position was not so much the result of his weakness of purpose and inability to take a decided step as an act in conformity with previous understandings arrived at with Caesar and Crassus. It is perhaps not the least of Caesar's claims to statesmanship that he knew at this critical point of his career how to play a waiting game. He was checked at the beginning of 63, but merely to proceed along fresh lines. He was even checked again at the beginning of 62, but, with the praetorship in his hands, a provincial governorship in prospect, financial support from Crassus, and an understanding with Pompey, he could endure passing mortifications, feeling confident that the goal for himself and his party was already within measurable distance of achievement.

INDEX

A

Actorius Naso, M., 18

Allobroges, envoys of, 73, 76, 77, 79

Antonius, C., stands for consulship, 24-29; elected, 30, 31; legislative proposals, 33; relations with Catiline and Cicero, 45, 47, 48; won over by Cicero, 70; marches against Catiline, 102

Apulia, 59

Arretium, 53, 70

Arrius, Q., 55, 56

Autronius Paetus, 5, 6, 12, 17, 25, 29, 34, 44, 46, 52, 74, 82, 110

B

Bestia, 75, 105

Bibulus, M., 16

C

Caecilius, L., 34

Caeparius, 77, 81

Caesar, C. Julius, political influence in 63, 1, 2; elected aedile, 5; part in first conspiracy, 17-20; aedile, 21; attempts to annex Egypt, 22; attitude to *sicarii*, 23; suspected of supporting Catiline, 24-29; acquits Catiline of murder, 32; plans for 63, 36, 37; *pontifex maximus*, 38; *praetor designatus*, 50; gives information to Cicero, 57, 58; supposed complicity, 82-84; attends debate of senate, 88; speech about punishment of conspirators, 91, 92; attitude with regard to executions, 98-101, 105, 106; accused by Vettius, 104; understanding with Pompey, 107-111

Capua, 59

Cassius Longinus, 25, 28, 74, 76, 78

Catiline, seeks consulship, 6; accused of *repetundae*, 6-11; first conspiracy, 12-20; acquitted of *repetundae*, 23; stands for consulship, 24-29; defeated, 30; secret intrigues, 31; hostility to Cicero, 31, 36; accused of murder, 32; again stands for consulship, 37, 39 seqq.; threatens violence, 40, 41, 42; is defeated, 45; collects band of conspirators, 51, 52, 53; accused under *Lex Plautia de vi*, 63; summons conspirators, 64; leaves Rome, 68; proclaimed a public enemy, 70; plan of action, 75; collapse, 101: destruction, 102

Cato, 41, 62, 72, 96, 97, 101, 103, 109

Catulus, Lutatius, 21, 22, 69, 83, 90, 104, 107

Cethegus, 25, 27, 52, 65, 72, 74, 76, 77, 79, 80, 81

Cicero, M. T., on Catiline's character, 8; promises to defend Manilius, 10; does not defend Catiline, 23; stands for consulship, 24; elected, 30; speech against Catiline, 32; opposes agrarian law, 34-36; carries *Lex Tullia*, 40; has elections postponed through fear of plots, 41-45; relations with Antonius, 47, 48; calls the senate, 55; his murder plotted, 65, 66; informed of conspiracy by Fulvia, 66; summons senate, 66; speech against Catiline, 66; gains loyalty of Antonius, 70; Metellus Celer, 71; obtains definite information of conspiracy, 73; has conspirators arrested, 77; makes them give evidence before senate, 77-80; speech to the people, 81; consults senate about punishment of conspirators, 85-89; speech in answer to Caesar, 95; has conspirators executed, 97; suspected of violating *Lex Porcia*, 98-101; increase of reputation, 103; attacked by Metellus Nepos, 105, 106; misjudges attitude of Caesar and Crassus, 110

Cicero, Quintus, 10, 28

Clodius, 8, 23, 69

Cornelius, 4, 9, 21, 65, 109

Cornificius, 81

Cotta, L., 6, 9, 10, 20, 90

Crassus, political influence in 63, 2-4; connection with Cornelius and Manilius, 4, 5; favours Catiline's candidature, 9; part in first conspiracy, 17-20; as censor, 21; suspected of supporting Catiline, 24-29; informs Cicero of conspiracy, 54, 65;